The
Mark Roth
Book of
BOWLING

The Mark Roth Book of BOWLING

by Mark Roth and Chuck Pezzano

Action photos of Mark Roth taken by Mel DiGiacomo

rP

The Rutledge Press
New York, New York

To our relatives and friends who have been so supportive over so many years. To the Professional Bowlers Association for the opportunity it gives to those who wish to make bowling a career. To the bowlers everywhere, beginners or superstars, who have made bowling the people's pastime.

Mark Roth
Chuck Pezzano
1981

Copyright © 1981 by The Rutledge Press

All rights reserved. No part of this book may be reproduced or transmitted in any form or by any means, electronic or mechanical, including photocopying, recording or by any information retrieval system, without permission in writing from the Publisher.

Published by The Rutledge Press, a division of W. H. Smith Publishers Inc.
112 Madison Avenue, New York, New York 10016

First Printing 1981
Printed in the United States of America
Library of Congress Cataloging in Publication Data

Pezzano, Chuck
  The Mark Roth book of bowling.

  1. Bowling. I. Roth, Mark. II. Title.
GV902.5.P495   794.6   81-10656
ISBN 0-8317-5800-7   AACR2

Acknowledgments

The wide-ranging bowling family has always been the most cooperative in every way, and so it was when certain needs had to be filled for this book. When the call went out for information, pictures, diagrams, and such, the answer was always yes.

Our appreciation for help and guidance is extended to Dr. George Allen, AMF; the American Bowling Congress; Joseph Antenora; Brunswick, Columbia Industries; Dave De Lorenzo; Frank and Ralph Esposito and their staff at Paramus Bowling; Jack Graziano; Steve James; John Jowdy; Harvey La Kind, who initiated the whole project; Larry Lichstein; Mort Luby, Jr.; Tom Kouros; Pepper Martin; the National Bowling Council; the Professional Bowlers Association; Jackie Roth; Art Serbo; Connie Smoot; Larry Weindruch; and Lyle Zikes.

And, of course, the easy-to-work-with Christy Polk, who coordinated the whole thing. Thanks, gang.

Contents

THE
MARK ROTH
RECORD

In 1977, 1978, and 1979 Mark Roth was named Bowler of the Year by the Bowling Writers Association of America. In the same years his fellow pros voted him the Sporting News Player of the Year honors. Roth has been an All-American selection from 1974 through 1980. The Metropolitan Bowling Writers Association (New York) has accorded him its highest tribute on seven occasions.

For the year ending 1980 Roth had won $657,343 in official money, second on the all-time list; and his unofficial bowling earnings and outside income made him a million-dollar bowler.

Among his most coveted records are eight tournament titles in a single year, most money won in a single year ($134,500), and most cashings in a row (51). The latter feat would stand in the same class as Joe DiMaggio's fabled 56-game hitting streak in baseball.

Four years in a row, 1976 through 1979, Roth won the George Young Memorial Award, which goes to the pro with the highest average for the year. In 1979 he chalked up the highest average ever, 221 plus. Roth has averaged better than 215 for some 10,000 pro games. Most bowlers won't roll that many games in a lifetime.

Roth has 17 perfect games in pro competition. He doesn't bother keeping a record of the 300s he rolls in practice or exhibitions. In addition to his 23 national tour wins as of the start of 1981, Roth had also captured four regional pro crowns, the Great and Greatest, Newsday Eastern Open, and dozens of city, county, state, and sectional titles.

Every pro dreams of the rare times he finishes high enough to roll on national television. Roth has appeared more than 100 times. In addition he's been featured on network shows such as *Fantasy Island, Battle of the Sexes,* and a number of sports specials.

Bowling is a sport in which age is not a tremendous factor, and many bowlers are just beginning to blossom in their twenties. Roth, before reaching the age of thirty, had already established his credentials for all-time greatness recognition. Following are the highlights of his professional career, year by year, with number of tournaments, money won, and top five finishes:

1970 (14) $1,132
1971 (10) $2,520

1972 (15) $12,103
Second, Chicago Brunswick World Open
1973 (22) $19,900
Third, Milwaukee Miller High Life Open
1974 (21) $36,879
Fourth, Arcadia, Calif., Don Carter Classic
Fourth, Las Vegas Showboat Invitational
Third, Kansas City King Louie Open
Second, Downey, Calif., PBA National Championship
Fifth, Chicago Brunswick World Open
1975 (24) $45,541
Winner, Kansas City King Louie Open
Second, Cleveland Copenhagen Open
Third, Downey, Calif., PBA National Championship
Fifth, Pittsburgh Open
Third, Battle Creek, Mich., Buzz Fazio Open
Fourth, Cleveland Canada Dry Open
1976 (28) $72,878
Second, Alameda, Calif., Open
Fifth, Kansas City King Louie Open
Third, Grand Prairie, Tex., BPAA U.S. Open
Winner, St. Louis Rolaids Open
Third, Tucson Open
Second, Cranston, R.I., New England Open
Winner; Pittsburgh Columbia 300 Open
Third, Battle Creek, Mich., Buzz Fazio Open
Winner, Cleveland Northern Ohio Open
Third, Hawaiian Invitational
1977 (28) $105,583
Third, Alameda, Calif., Ford Open
Winner, Las Vegas Showboat Invitational
Fourth, St. Louis Rolaids Open
Fifth, Palatine, Ill., Midas Open
Third, Miami Burger King Open
Winner, San Jose PBA Doubles Classic (with Marshall Holman)
Winner, Fresno Open
Winner, Norwalk, Calif., Southern California Open
Second, Tucson Open
Second, New England Open
Second, Reading, Pa., AMF Regional Champions Classic
Fifth, Cleveland Northern Ohio Open
Second, Chicago Brunswick World Open
Second, Detroit AMF Grand Prix

1978 (26) $134,500

Winner, Torrance, Calif., Lite Classic
Winner, Grand Prairie, Tex., Quaker State Open
Winner, Kansas City King Louie Open
Third, Miami Burger King Open
Third, Garden City, N.Y., Long Island Open
Winner, Greater Hartford Open
Fourth, Akron, Ohio, Firestone Tournament of Champions
Third, Seattle Columbia-PBA Doubles Classic (with Marshall Holman)
Third, Reno PBA National Championship
Winner, Portland Open
Winner, San Jose Open
Winner, New England Open
Winner, Rochester, N.Y., Brunswick Regional Champions Classic
Second, Cleveland Northern Ohio Open
Second, Reno AMF Grand Prix

1979 (26) $124,517

Fourth, Las Vegas Showboat Invitational
Second, Grand Prairie, Tex., Quaker State Open
Third, San Antonio, Tex., AMF MagicScore Open
Winner, St. Louis Rolaids Open
Winner, Kansas City King Louie Open
Third, Garden City, N.Y., Long Island Open
Winner, San Jose, Calif., Columbia-PBA Doubles Classic (with Marshall Holman)
Fifth, Las Vegas PBA National Championship
Winner, Portland Open
Fifth, Fresno Open
Second, Rochester, N.Y., Brunswick Regional Champions Classic
Winner, Indianapolis Kessler Classic
Winner, Cleveland Lawson's Open
Third, Syracuse Open

1980 (28) $101,665

Fourth, Alameda, Calif., Open
Second, Las Vegas Showboat Invitational
Second, Garden City, N.Y., Long Island Open
Second, Milwaukee Miller High Life Open
Second, Las Vegas PBA Doubles Classic (with Marshall Holman)
Fourth, Portland Open

Third, Fresno U.S. Polychemical Open
Fifth, Torrance Southern California Open
Fourth, Buffalo Open
Winner, Rochester, N.Y., Brunswick Regional Champions
     Classic
Fifth, Indianapolis Kessler Classic
Second, Louisville, Ky., ABC Masters

Donna Adamek and Mark Roth are all smiles after scoring wins. They dominated bowling in the late 1970s, each being named a three-time Bowler of the Year.

WHO IS
MARK ROTH,
by Mark Roth

I like to think of myself as just an average guy who hit it lucky. Growing up in Brooklyn I was involved in many sports, mostly of the street variety. We had our forms of hockey, my favorite being roller hockey, played on skates, with few hits or holds barred and survival being the main goal. To this day I love hockey and live and die with the New York Rangers.

I played a lot of school-yard basketball, some regular baseball, and, of course, plenty of stick ball, with whatever was available used in the way of equipment. When all you need is something to hit with and something to hit at, you don't have to search too far. From the time I can remember, I went into things all the way. I always felt if it wasn't worth doing your best, then it wasn't worth doing.

We weren't poor, because we didn't know what poor meant. We ate, had a warm place to sleep, and could hang around as much as we wanted. My father died when I was young, so my mother and sister guided me most of the way. I wasn't brilliant in school, but I wasn't the worst, either.

I guess I was about eleven when they put up a bowling center a few blocks away from where I lived. I had bowled a few times and liked it. But when I got to bowl more, I just fell in love with the sport. I couldn't wait to knock those pins down, and I did it the best way I knew how. I wasn't scientific, but I was eager and enthusiastic, as excited as an explorer who has just discovered another new world.

Soon I learned that it cost money to bowl, so I went to work in the bowling center. I cleaned the floor, the pins, the ash trays, the carpets, and even the rest rooms. And I used the money I earned to bowl and bowl and bowl.

The owner was good to me because he saw how interested I was, so he let me bowl at discount rates and then moved me up, teaching me to be a pin chaser and then a mechanic. I enjoyed that, and to this day, when I visit my friends who own bowling centers, I'll gladly jump into the pits to help fix a machine that isn't working right. I've done that on tour, too.

But that's just a diversion. My profession is bowling. Once I started to bowl and watched the pros on TV winning what I considered a fabulous fortune of $3,000 in a single tournament, I swore that was the way I was going to make my living. I would have been more than satisfied just to make ends meet. Even as a youngster I found I could win against kids my own age and most who were a lot older. In our teens we bowled for a few dollars in pot games where everyone tossed in a dollar or two and the winner took it all. Once in a while the stakes would get higher, and it gave me a lift to win so often.

Then I discovered there were so-called amateur tournaments in which you could win money. It was like I discovered gold, and I spent most of my weekends bowling.

It was only natural for me to move on to try the pro tour. After all, my big interest was bowling; the only work I had done was connected with bowling; and I did show some talent in it. I didn't win at first, but I made enough money to stay afloat and remain independent. Once I found out I could win, the feeling fed on itself. I wanted to win more and more. Before I'm through I want to be considered the greatest bowler who ever lived.

I don't consider myself a nasty person, but when I bowl against someone, whether it's a friend, a roommate, a doubles partner, or even my wife or mother, they aren't what they are anymore until the game is over. They become a challenger, an enemy, someone to beat. Once the game or match is over, all is forgotten until the next time. It may not be the right way for everyone, but it's my way.

I also know I've been accused of being uncooperative before and after matches or tournaments. If I am guilty it's because I value my bowling so highly. Before I start a tournament, I psych myself up for what is coming; and when it's over, I'm beat, physically and mentally. I'm always thinking back and ahead, back to what I did so I can learn by it, ahead so that I can do better in the future.

In my own way, I respect and like almost everyone in bowling— my fellow bowlers, the officials from the PBA and other organizations, and press people, too. I guess I've been misquoted too often or take to heart some of the things I hear. I don't want to be a Greta Garbo, but I dearly love my privacy as well as I love my sport. I know I wouldn't and couldn't be where I am if it weren't for the pioneering pros, the officials, the sponsors, the newspaper, radio, and TV people.

And I try to be reasonable in my own framework. If I haven't been, it hasn't been on purpose and I'll keep trying, the same as I did playing on the streets in Brooklyn or when I decided that bowling was for me, even if that ball seemed so big and heavy.

WHO IS
MARK ROTH,
by Chuck Pezzano

Mark Roth was an exciting bowler from the first day he tossed a bowling ball, using both hands and taking ten steps to get to the line. Soon after getting into competition, he was rated among the best in Brooklyn, and as a teenager, one of the best in the East. Before he could vote he had drawn national attention; and as a young man in his twenties, he rated with the best in the world. Now the only question is where Roth will place in the history of the sport. Assured of one of the upper niches, number one is the one he desires most.

It is probable that although he, indeed, realizes he is a great bowler, Mark Roth has never been able to accept the fact that he is a celebrity, a personality.

What is often mistaken for ego or aloofness on his part is more likely bashfulness. What is charged as disinterest or discourteous action could well be an inability to comprehend why there is such interest in someone who merely tosses this round object at those bottle-shaped objects and manages to knock them down so much better than so many other millions.

Roth still feels uncomfortable in large crowds, or even small crowds. He prefers to sit off in the corner rather than being the life of the party, or even one of its sparks. Wherever he goes, the spotlight naturally falls on him.

He's as intense a person as you will ever meet yet tries to cling to a childlike simplicity. In interviews he is often cautious with his answers about everything but his bowling. There he is in his element and tells it how he feels. He tends to look for hidden motives in questions and actions of others, because along the way he has learned too much the hard way.

Roth is comfortable with people he knows well, people he has been around a long time.

When he first began to bowl well, he had terrible trouble with his bowling thumb. It was a swollen mass of lumps, callused, often pock-marked with the scars of previous battles. It bled and it became infected, and it was ugly and grotesque. But it made for good copy; and, believe it or not, Mark Roth's thumb, looking more like a butcher's mistake, was featured full screen on national television.

Looking back it is easy to see why Roth was perturbed when he

14

Before competing Mark Roth checks out the action with his wife, Jackie. He pauses for a long puff, strolls on the beach, and smiles after a good outing on the lanes. All candids from Jackie's album.

plaintively noted, "Some writers write more about my thumb than they do about my bowling. And some people should realize that there is a person attached to the thumb."

Failing to understand some things that went on, the youthful Roth became even more intense in his bowling. If his mother was stretched out on the approach or lane, he'd find a way to hook the ball around her and get a strike.

Roth is one of the best-known and easily recognized personalities in sports. He can't walk through an airport, shop in a supermarket, or stroll down a street without requests for autographs or a word or two. A typical tourist, he loves to make the rounds of the amusement parks or the local attractions when he's on the road. He thoroughly enjoyed a tour of Universal Studios, and gladly posed for pictures and answered all questions. This was Mark Roth far from the terror of the lanes and the image of a man who stands aside when crowds gather.

Maybe he'll always have a lot of kid in him. He still loves sports and was thrilled when he attended a hockey game and a puck came flying into the stands right into his hands. He loves to tinker and tamper with vehicles of all sorts, and has a keen interest in model trains, particularly the older ones.

He moved from Brooklyn to Staten Island to the New Jersey shore, and often he races across the sand with the dog he and wife, Jackie treasure, long-haired, jet-black Bozo. Watch him in that atmosphere and you can see the feeling of relaxation build, away from the worry of whether a pin goes down or not or whether the glare of the TV lights is too bright.

In most sports you can't see the athlete because his uniform and equipment cover and hide his body and much of his face. But a bowler such as Roth, on national TV from six to ten times a year, often full face for an hour or more almost becomes part of the family to the 20 million faithful viewers watching.

Roth is comfortable financially, and the odds are that he has another 20 years of top earnings ahead of him. His place in bowling history is firm. But in many ways he is still the same kid who always had to find a way to solve his roller hockey or stick-ball problems on the rough, tough streets of Brooklyn.

Some used fists to fight their way up, others books, but Mark Roth chose bowling balls at 60 feet and he handles them as deftly as a microsurgeon does the delicate tools of his trade.

Roth checks a score with newsman Jerry Levine, shows his battered thumb, and proudly displays his jogging partner, the Roth's family dog, who doesn't bowl.

17

FRAME

1

PROFESSIONAL BOWLING— THE NEW KID ON THE SPORTS BLOCK

Each year some new professional sports enterprise is hailed as the possible rage of the coming decade. But rolling on year after year is one of the youngest of the many sports on the American scene, professional bowling. Few thought it would survive its formative years, and fewer still predicted its continuing success.

Almost from the start of organized bowling, back in 1895, attempts were made to form bowlers into various types of pro groups, including the ill-fated National Bowling League, which folded in less than a year after a most ambitious attempt to establish it in 1960.

Team bowling was the thing, and the bowlers who could loosely be called pros, those who made their living through the sport, were sponsored by commercial firms, mostly breweries, and centered in the then hot-beds of bowling; Chicago, St. Louis, and Detroit.

That all changed in 1958 when an Akron, Ohio, attorney named Eddie Elias, amazed when he discovered there was no such thing as a professional bowling organization, talked 33 founding charter members into forming the Professional Bowlers Association of America.

Elias, who also served as the host of a TV show, had always been blessed with a love of sports, had a large dose of show business in his blood, and a gift for selling and promotion. He was truthful when he laid out his plans, promising mostly an opportunity for talented keglers to perform for a living much as the golf tourists did.

In 1959 there were three tournaments and $49,500 in prize money. Five years later there were 31 events worth $1,200,000. The prize money continued to grow, bolstered by added commercial sponsors and TV revenue, and reached $2 million for the first time in 1970, then broke the $3-million barrier in the late 1970s. Steady but solid increases are projected through the century.

Membership soared from the original 33 who took a gamble to more than 2,000 of the world's greatest bowlers hailing from every state and a number of foreign countries. Bowling is growing throughout the world, and more than 60 countries participate in official amateur bowling events. Each country is moving to the day when its best can compete with the Americans. Japan has its own pro organization, and representatives from more than 20 countries participate in pro events each year.

An extensive regional program offers weekend pros and teaching pros the opportunity to keep their regular jobs and still compete in top-flight action. There are some 90 regional events offering more than a million dollars in prize money, a good place for the aspiring pro to

DON JOHNSON   EARL ANTHONY   DICK WEBER

Pictured are three of the sport's best— Vesma Grinfelds, Carol Anderton, and Judy Soutar. PBA Hall of Famers Don Johnson, Earl Anthony, and Dick Weber. Former rookie of the year, top pro Steve Neff. Opposite: A determined Wayne Webb, 1980 Bowler of the Year.

start and the veteran to return to when he tires of the national tour.

In 1980 every one of the PBA's national stops were nationally televised, and ABC-TV's Pro Bowlers Tour went into its twentieth straight year in 1981 as one of the longest-running and highest-rated TV sports shows in the history of television.

The nerve center of the PBA is the home office in Akron, Ohio, where commissioner Joseph Antenora and his home office staff guide the destiny of the PBA. Almost half of the full-time group of 20 are on the road most of the time, tending to the needs of the tour, conducting the events, and aiding with lane maintenance, publicity, and promotion.

In addition, six regional directors and more than 100 volunteer members, serving in various capacities as members of the Executive Board, Tournament Committee, and many other committees, help keep the PBA alive and moving forward.

Pro bowling has problems few other sports have faced, much less overcome. Bowling centers, the stadiums of bowling except on rare occasions when brand new lanes are constructed in arenas or other type of stadia, are the homes of bowling tournaments but were erected strictly as commercial enterprises, with little or no permanent

spectator seating or facilities to answer to the other needs associated with spectator sports. Thus, when a pro event is staged, temporary bleachers, locker rooms, press rooms, and other facilities taken for granted in sports arenas must be carefully planned and constructed.

Most pro events draw well, but the total paid gates fall far short of other sports simply because there isn't enough room. Space available ranges from an average of about 1,200 to 3,000 seats in the more spacious centers.

A bowling pro, unlike a football player, a baseball player, or most other athletes, is engaged in a sport in which almost everyone can participate. Making it more difficult on him is the fact that the best one can do in bowling is to score a strike, knock all ten pins down with a single ball. By skill, or sheer luck or mistake, practically anyone of any age, size, or physical strength can score a single strike. The fact is that bowling is one of the simplest sports to learn to do, but one of the most difficult to master.

As a kid I watched TV and was fooled because I could roll a strike or two and once in a while come up with games better than the pros shot on TV. In fact, as I got better, I would write down the scores they rolled on TV, then go out and practice and match my scores against theirs; and if I bowled long enough, I'd always manage to win.

But to achieve success as a pro you must be able to chalk up strikes with unbelievable regularity (six to eight strikes a game). The difference between the amateur or casual side of the sport and the professional class is roughly the same as the difference between a touch football game at a company or family picnic and the type of football played by those teams making it to the Super Bowl.

The pros are the showcase for the millions of bowlers in this country, and they set the pace in style, technique, and equipment. But it's no piece of cake for them. Each year more than a hundred aspiring pros set out to make it big. Since they were tots they have watched pro bowling on TV. They have gone through the junior, school, and semi-pro ranks and most of them are the best in their area. Yet only a handful will survive. Most are not fully prepared, and I'd like to tell them some of what they can expect.

Every young bowler has confidence in his ability and I think it helps to be a little cocky, but common sense is just as important if you're thinking about a pro career. And the first item in that area is finances.

Expenses are high, as much as $600 to $800 weekly to cover entry fees, travel, food, lodging, equipment, and incidentals. Many pro bowlers are sponsored, by commercial enterprises looking for the exposure, by bowling centers, by their families, or their friends.

These three pros have won the most prestigious titles in the sport. Mike Durbin is a Firestone champion, Joey Berardi has won the BPAA U.S. Open, and Eddie Ressler captured the ABC Masters crown. All three consistently place in the top 20 money winners each year. Opposite: World famous trick-shot artist Andy Varipapa at age 86.

23

If none of the above are readily available, and in most cases they aren't for a young, untried bowler, then the bowler must sponsor himself, or, as Hall-of-Famer Billy Hardwick did, sell shares in himself, with all shareholders profiting or losing based on the bowler's cashing performance.

In any kind of sponsorship or corporate setup, there should be no questions and everything should be in writing so that there are no misunderstandings. In many cases, people who sponsor a bowler do it because they are sporting-minded persons and want to give a youngster a break. But should that youngster break loose and win more than $100,000 in a year, then it better be on a business understanding.

Normally, the bowler is allowed a set weekly amount to cover all his expenses. That amount is deducted first from any prize money he wins, and what remains is the profit, to be distributed on the predetermined percentages, ranging from a 50–50 split to as much as 90–10, with the bowler always receiving the larger cut of the pie.

There have been some great sponsors in bowling. One in particular sponsored about half-a-dozen bowlers. He said he used to bet on horses and lose a lot of money, and this way he was getting the same thrill and the same action and still giving some bowlers a shot at

Jim Godman is known as the Tarzan of the tour because of his great strength as shown by the way he handles a bowling ball, supporting the full weight in a unique delivery. Paul Colwell was one of the first pros to win a major title using an angle from the left of the center of the lane. Opposite: Hall of Famer Wayne Zahn.

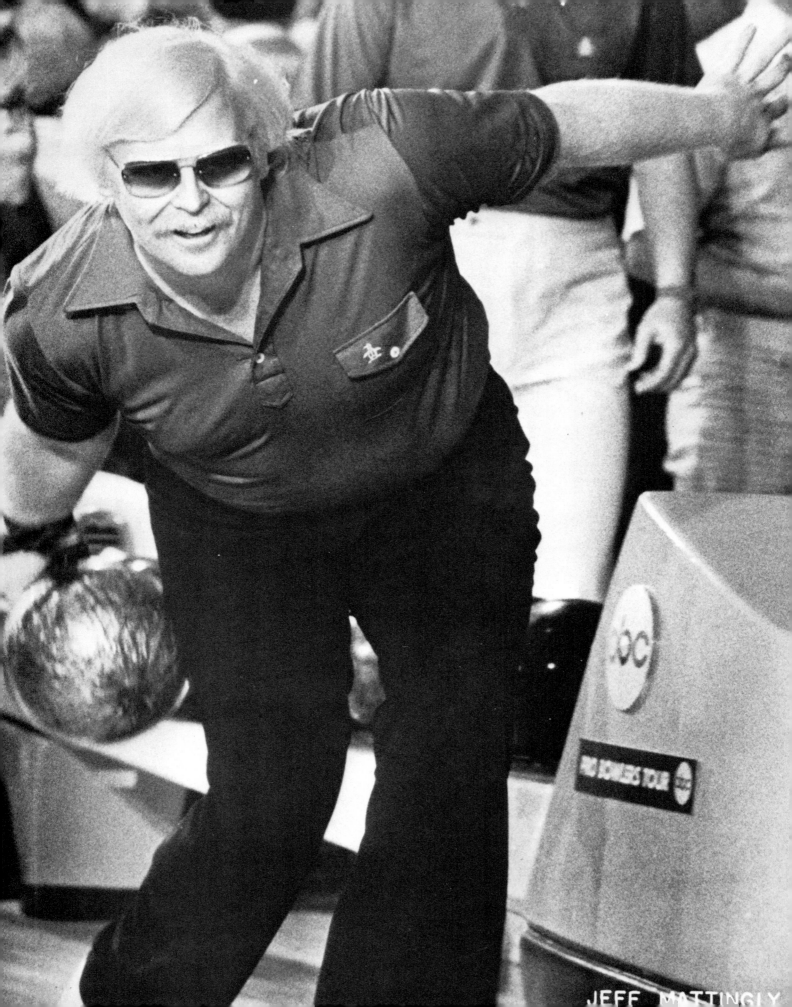

fame and fortune. I asked him if there was any difference in sponsoring bowlers and owning and betting on horses.

"One big one," he replied. "I always knew where the horses were the night before a race."

I emphasize financing because a new pro should be prepared to last three to six months, preferably a year, to give himself the proper chance. There have been few overnight sensations in bowling—it's just too tough. The tension of a new experience, added to the competitive pressure of the bowling are enough to worry about without the fear of where your next meal or entry fee is coming from. If you really want to bowl, you can work awhile, or even borrow the money to give you a start. Once the finances have been settled, you must concentrate on your game.

Mike Aulby, Rookie of the Year in 1979, rolled in as many different bowling centers as he could in his home area to get used to all kinds of lane conditions. I have some friends who own lanes, so I will often practice by setting up various lane conditions on different lanes in the same center. Remember, on tour you bowl in a different city in a different bowling center and move from lane to lane after each game, so you will run into almost every conceivable type of lane condition.

Equipment can drive you nuts, and you will find much detail in the chapter about bowling balls; but in a nutshell, make sure you have the basic equipment, and make sure you have a fellow bowler or pro shop expert who knows about equipment to help you.

The main thing is to have an open mind about your game. Have the courage to stick with it until you're sure it won't work and then have the good sense to make adjustments as needed. Every bowler should first bowl the way he or she likes to bowl best. From there the adjustments should always be to a simpler way, less hook, more accuracy, straighter arm swing and so on—actually a return to the basics. A valuable tool to a beginning pro, and to any pro, is the use of video tape. Watch yourself closely, and do it often. Almost every time I'm home from tour, whether for a day or month, I take a good look at myself.

You must be master of your own game; but apart from the bowling itself, it also pays to keep in good physical shape, and to me the legs are the key, as they are in almost all sports. Walking, jogging, running, bike riding, and any of the many leg exercises you can do in a gym, at home or in a hotel room will be very helpful.

If you can, before you go on tour, get into the best local competition you can, whether it be in matches, league play, or tournaments. Always try to get in a little over your head. If you're the best in your area, go to neighboring cities or states. I've found there are more

Jeff Mattingly, a thrilling pro who rolls one of the most devastating balls. Affectionately known as the Great White Whale.

than enough good bowlers everywhere.

It might come as a great shock to some new pros when they find they just can't step into the big money tournaments by filing an entry, but often must earn their way in through the pro tour qualifying, better known as the *rabbit squads* of pro events.

Because there are so many bowlers wanting to bowl in each tournament and the number of lanes and the number of days limit the number of contestants, the PBA has come up with the fairest method to determine who bowls.

Past champions, players finishing in the finals the week before, players who finished in the top 50 in point performance standings the previous year, and bowlers who rate high in career point listings are exempt from qualifying.

For instance, in a field of 160 bowlers, there may be 80 exempt players, leaving 80 spots for the qualifiers. The rabbits, sometimes as many as 200, roll in the pretournament qualifying to determine who wins the spots in the tournament proper.

Therefore, a new pro must prove he is good enough just to get into the tournament proper. This procedure has created a new group in pro bowling called the *touring rabbits*.

A regular pro tournament starts with a pro–amateur tournament on Tuesday. This is when the local junior bowlers and local amateurs get a chance to roll with the pros as partners. Pro-ams are very popular, drawing as many as 1,500 entries in some cities. Try a pro–am, and don't be afraid to talk to the pro. You will find most of them happy to answer any question you might have, as long as it isn't too personal.

The tournament proper starts on Wednesday, each of the contestants rolling 12 games, in two blocks of six games. Another six games are rolled by every bowler in the field on Thursday. Then the field is cut to the high 24 scorers based on total pins for 18 games. The 24 survivors return for eight games of match play Thursday night, then two more rounds of eight games each on Friday. In the match play the bowlers roll against each other, and the winner of each match receives a 30-pin bonus for winning. By the end of Friday night the bowlers have rolled 42 games, and the field is reduced to the top five, who return on Saturday for the televised finals.

The TV stepladder format features four games. In the first, the fifth-place finisher meets number four, winner goes against three, victor against number two, and the winner meets the leading qualifier for the one game to decide the championship.

Few athletes in any sport are called upon to meet such a demanding schedule. The pro bowler is in actual competition more than eight hours a day for three straight days. He could well be tied up for 12

Matt Surina, one of the best in the Northwest, Guppy Troup, born in Scotland, Bill Spigner, a fine teacher, and Ernie "USA" Schlegel, the man of uniforms.

29

Bowling beauty Betty Morris, named Bowler of the Decade, is surrounded by solid stars Roy Buckley, Jay Robinson, Alvin Lou, and lefty Paul Moser, all champions on the national tour. Morris bowled against Mark Roth on TV in a battle of the sexes. She lost the single game.

30

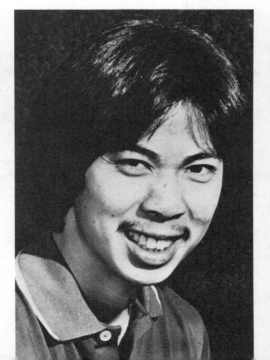

to 15 hours with going back and forth to the lanes, and then he must face the pressure of TV.

What it means to the newcomer is that he must change his entire previous lifestyle. Eating, sleeping, and bowling habits must be changed to conform to life on the tour. I usually eat a light breakfast and never more than a sandwich and maybe soup between squads. Never overeat. My big meal is usually when the action is over, which means I often eat a steak at midnight. And I often have breakfast early in the afternoon.

I like to watch TV during a tournament because I like TV and it relaxes me, takes my mind away from the business. It's important to be able to relax because the mental side of bowling is just as tough, if not tougher, than the physical side. I'm fortunate in that I earn enough so that if I want to fly home between stops or if I don't make the cut, I can afford it. There is nothing like home to calm you, bring you down to earth. Many pros can't afford the extra expense, so they practice, develop hobbies or business activities they can work on the road. I also enjoy sporting events and tourist spots. Others go to the movies a lot or play cards or read.

The tour certainly has some glamour, but there is more hard work and adjustment than excitement. The travel is constant. Many pros travel by motor homes, others by van or car or plane.

Motor homes or vans are popular because they can hold so many bowling balls. Did you ever try to check in 12 bowling balls at an airport? The PBA has a players' services director who has huge vehicles to carry the bowling balls and shirts of the pros from stop to stop. It's up to you to travel by whatever mode is best for you and your pocketbook. It's important to make and keep friends. Some bowlers don't make it, not because they lack the ability but because they couldn't adjust to the traveling, the living out of a suitcase, and just plain loneliness.

The way to look at it is that each week is a new tournament, a new city, a new bowling center, new people, and a new experience, one that will stay with you even if you never make a dent as a pro bowler. I have seen many successful pros, and many more who didn't make it; but I've never met a bowler who was sorry he gave it a try.

In summing up, don't be afraid but do be curious; don't have preconceived notions but try to learn as much as you can before you go on tour. Most of all, be totally prepared for a new bowling life against bowlers you never realized could be so good and knowledgeable; but remember, they all started just like you.

As one spectator noted, "I think these guys could average 220 rolling in the parking lot, against trees."

FRAME

2

UNDERSTANDING THE TALK OF THE GAME—
Bowling Terms.

ABC—American Bowling Congress, official rule-making and sanctioning body of the sport of tenpin bowling.

Address—Bowler's starting position; also called *stance.*

AJBC—American Junior Bowling Congress.

Alley—Early designation of playing surface, now more commonly called *lane.*

Anchor—Final player in team's line-up.

Approach—Area behind foul line along which player makes move to deliver ball. Also, the actual physical act of moving to the foul line.

Arrows—Targeting devices imbedded in lane.

Baby ball—A ball that is released too carefully.

Baby split—The 2–7 or 3–10 spare leaves.

Backup—A ball that fades to the right for a right-hander and to the left for a left-hander.

Bed—Alley or lane.

Bedposts—The 7–10 split.

Belly—To aim and roll the ball in a wide arc from the center of the lane away from the pocket area, but imparting enough hook to bring it back sharply into the pocket.

Big fill—Knocking down eight or nine pins on a spare or a double strike.

Big four—The 4–6–7–10 split; also known as *double pinochle.*

Blind—A frame or game score given a team when a team member is late or absent, based on the missing player's average or an amount set by the league.

Block—A group of games in a tournament. Play is divided into blocks.

Blocked lane—One treated with a build up of oil or lane dressing to create a path or track, usually to the pocket to make scoring easier, usually illegal under ABC rules.

Blow—A miss; failure to score a strike or spare; an error.

Blow the rack—An impressive-looking strike because all pins seem to go down as one.

Boards—Individual pieces of wood used to construct a lane.

Body English—Movement after the ball has been delivered in an attempt to steer it or help knock the pins down.

Box—A single frame.

BPAA—Bowling Proprietors Association of America, the trade association of owners of bowling centers.

Bridge—Distance separating bowling ball finger holes.

Brooklyn—A first ball that hits to the left of the head pin when rolled by a right-hander and to the right when rolled by a left-hander.

Bucket—A difficult spare leave of the 2–4–5–8 for a righty and 3–5–6–

9 for a lefty; also called *dinner bucket* or *pail.*

Channel—More recent name for gutter, the depression on both sides of the lane to catch errant tosses and guide them to pit.

Chop—Knocking down the front pin or pins on a spare leave without making the spare; also referred to as a *cherry.*

Clean game—Achieving a strike or a spare in each frame.

Clothesline—The 1–2–4–7 or 1–3–6–10 spare leaves; also known as the *fence* or *picket fence.*

Count—Number of pins knocked down on first ball.

Cranker—Any bowler who throws a wide and sharp breaking hook ball.

Dead ball—A ball released so badly that it has no drive, may bounce a bit; and when it contacts the pins deflects excessively and is very ineffective.

Deuce—A 200 game or 200 average.

Dodo—A ball declared illegal because it is over the weight limit or is improperly balanced.

Double wood—Pins directly behind one another, 2–8, 3–9, etc.

Dutch 200—An even 200 game accomplished by alternating strikes and spares.

Fill—Pins knocked down when working on a spare or double strike.

Foul—Going beyond the foul line in any way. Penalty is loss of the results of the ball rolled.

Foul line—Black marking separating beginning of lane from end of approach.

Foundation—A strike in 9th frame.

Frame—One-tenth of a game.

Fudge—A weak shot producing a weak ball, on purpose to cut down a hook, or else the result of poor ball release.

Full hit—When the ball makes contact with the head pin near its center; also called high or tight hit.

Greek church—Split leave when three pins remain standing on one side and two on the other, because the pins resemble church steeples.

Gutter shot—Technique developed by pros of rolling ball from extreme edge of lane, usually the first inch.

Handicap—Pins awarded to lower average teams or individuals in an attempt to equalize competition.

Head pin—The front or number 1 pin in the setup.

Heads—The front portion of the lane from the foul line to the 16-foot mark.

Hole—Another name for the strike pocket; also another name for a *split.*

34

House—Bowling center.

House ball—Bowling balls supplied free by bowling center.

Inside—Toward the center of the lane, usually referring to position where ball is released.

Jersey—An opposite pocket hit, 1–2 for right-handers, 1–3 for lefties.

Kegler—Another name for bowler.

Kickbacks—Sideboards at end of lane from which pins often bounce back on lane.

Kingpin—The number 5 pin.

Lane—Playing surface.

Leadoff—First bowler in a team line-up.

Leave—Pins left standing after first ball.

Lift—Upward motion with fingers at point of ball release.

Line—Path ball takes; also a single game of bowling.

Lofting—Throwing the ball out over the foul line, causing it to hit with a jolt or bounce, rather than rolling it smoothly.

Maples—Bowling pins.

Mark—Strike or spare.

Match play—Competition in which bowlers roll against each other.

Medal play—Competition in which only total pins count, no match play.

Mixer—A ball rolled with enough action to cause the pins to spin and bounce around when hit.

Nose hit—A ball hitting the pins dead center.

Open—A frame without a strike or spare recorded.

Outside—Angle from right or left of lane, not as extreme as gutter shot, usually 3rd to 10th boards.

PBA—Professional Bowlers Association.

Pie—A lane on which it is easy to score; also called *soft.*

Pitch—Angles at which bowling ball holes are drilled; also could describe method of tossing ball, as in baseball pitch.

Pocket—The strike zone, 1–3 for righties, 1–2 for lefties.

Poodle—A gutter ball.

Punch out—To end a game from any given point with all strikes.

Railroad—A split.

Rap—Pin remaining standing on what seems to be a perfect hit; also called *tap, touch, burner.*

Reach—Extension of bowling arm to bring ball well out on lane, across foul line.

Rolloff—Special match or contest to break a tie.

Runway—Starting area, approach.

Sanctioned—Competition in accordance with American Bowling Congress or Women's International Bowling Congress rules.

One of the keys to good bowling is the ability to reach out to get the ball well over the foul line. Notice how far both Roth's arm and the ball extend toward the pins.

Sandbagger—Bowler who purposely keeps average down to receive a higher handicap.

Scratch—Actual score, no handicap.

Sleeper—One pin hidden behind another; also called *barmaid.*

Slots—High scoring lanes.

Sour apple—Weak hitting ball, one that leaves the rare 5–7–10 split.

Span—Distance between inner edges of thumb and finger holes.

Spare—When all pins are downed with two balls.

Split—A spare leave in which the head pin is down and two or more pins are left standing with a pin down immediately between or

ahead of them causing a gap.

Spot—Target area on approach or lane.

Stiff—A lane that does not allow a ball to hook easily.

Strike—Knocking all ten pins down with the first ball of a frame.

String—Consecutive strikes, usually three or more.

Track—Area most used on lane, creating a path to pins; also area on a bowling ball where it rolls and picks up minute particles.

Turkey—Three strikes in a row.

Washout—The 1–2–10, 1–2–4–10, 1–3–7, 1–3–6–7 spare leaves.

WIBC—Women's International Bowling Congress.

FRAME

3

EQUIPMENT

At the Lanes

When you visit a bowling center, whether it is in your home town or any other town, whether the population is 5,000 or 5 million, you can rest assured that the equipment will be standardized if the lanes are approved and sanctioned by the American Bowling Congress, as almost 100 percent are. The ABC is the official rule-making body of the sport along with its sister organization, the Women's International Bowling Congress.

When you step on the approach of a modern lane and set into action all the factors needed for you to bowl, you're entering into an expensive world, costing as much as $30,000 per lane.

Construction techniques are similar, and though all lanes look the same and may be of the same dimensions, lane and scoring conditions are vastly different. This is because different lane dressings, varied patterns of conditioners, and different ways of conditioning by different people or machines can all cause great variances. Add to that the vast differences in the material used to make the lanes. Since the wood comes from different trees and reacts differently in the varying climates and treatment it receives, there can be no such thing as a uniform lane condition all the time in every center.

The *lane* is the playing surface in bowling. It measures 62 feet, 10¾ inches from the foul line to the pit. The *foul line,* akin to boundary lines in other sports, is the black-colored divider signaling the end of the approach, the walking and striding area a bowler uses to reach the playing area, and the actual playing surface where the ball rolls.

The distance from the foul line to the center of the number 1, or head pin is 60 feet. Most approaches are 16 feet. Though some are slightly shorter, they must be at least 15 feet. The approach and first portion of the lane, called the *heads,* covering some 16 feet down the lane, are constructed of sturdy wood, usually hard rock maple.

The area from that point to the pin deck, approximately an additional 44 feet, the merging areas distinguished by the dove-tail grooving, is constructed of pine, a softer wood.

The *pin deck,* the flat area where the pins are placed, is also maple or some strong synthetic material. The harder, sturdier wood or other material is needed up front and down back at the end, because those are the areas taking the most physical abuse, the high-traffic areas.

The approach takes all of the bowler's walking, running, and pounding; and the heads must absorb the landing of the ball. The pin deck area takes the constant contact of ball against pins, pins bouncing against each other and hitting the deck, and, of course, the necessary motion of the machines that set the pins.

The width of the playing portion of the lane is 41½ inches with a tolerance of ½ inch, so it can range between 41 and 42 inches. For the channels, or *gutters,* on each side to catch the bad balls, add 9¼ to 9⅜ inches for an overall width of 60 inches, give or take ½ inch.

Each wooden lane is constructed of hand-selected, choice boards, 39 in all, 38 usually exact in size, a fraction more than an inch, and the thirty-ninth to make up the difference to get to regulation size.

Located in the approach area and on the playing surface are a series of targeted devices. On the approach there are three rows of dots, one at the foul line at about 2 inches behind, another row at the 12-foot mark, and still another group at the 15-foot distance.

Dots are imbedded into the lane on the 3, 5, 8, 11, and 14 boards 7 feet down the lane.

The targets, called *arrows, darts, marks, diamonds, triangles, designs,* or whatever, mostly arrows, are located on the 5, 10, 15, and 20 boards. They are staggered from 13 feet plus to a little more than 15 feet from the foul line.

Pros always talk in arrows or boards. I've explained the arrows. For a right-hander the first board on the right is the number 1 board; and the numbers go up to the center board, which is board number 20. A left-hander would start his count from the left, with the first board on

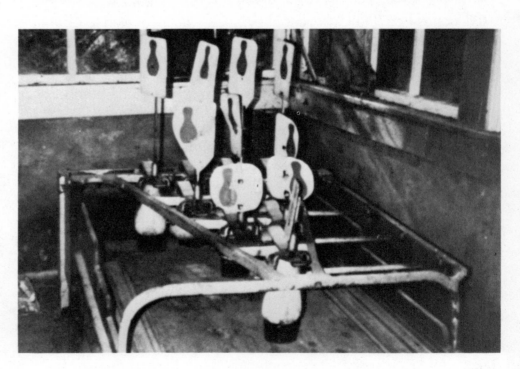

After releasing his ball Mark Roth quickly moved to the left in this photo to give the viewer a look at the general line of a ball rolled between the second and third arrows on the lane, normally a good starting target area for all bowlers. Note the ball has just passed the spot. *Opposite: Equipment used in a bowling game in the 1930s.*

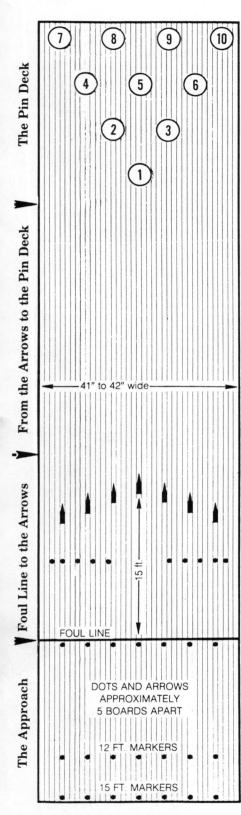

41″ to 42″ wide

15 ft.

FOUL LINE

DOTS AND ARROWS
APPROXIMATELY
5 BOARDS APART

12 FT. MARKERS

15 FT. MARKERS

42

the left being his number 1 board and his numbers would rise until reaching the common number 20 board.

I do not include all these measurements, dimensions, and lane markings as trivia information but to point out that bowling is as precise a game as you want it to be. The dots and arrows aren't there to dress up the lanes; they are to be used as guides to give you starting and finishing points on the approach, so you will be able to watch your ball go over other markings on the lane and adjust.

There is no great need to try to remember lane statistics, but a deeper look at them reveals that some keen scientific and mathematical thinking went into creating these dimensions so that the sport would be a challenge and yet not be so difficult as to discourage all but the strong or brave.

Though today's lane is a marvel of engineering, far from primitive, it should be pointed out that the 60-foot distance from foul line to head pin is the same distance natives in the South Seas used when they engaged in their own brand of bowling thousands of years ago. And wood is still the primary material for lanes though it was first used as early as the thirteenth century.

There are various synthetics in use, and many more in various experimental stages. Granite approaches have been tried. Coatings atop the current wood, solid blocks to replace the wood, and combinations of numerous materials loom in the future. Though wood lanes figure to be around a long time, the fine wood used for lanes grows scarcer, wood needs careful and special treatment, and maintenance costs are a factor. When the results are in on synthetics that will last longer, be easier to maintain, and look as great as wood, then wood will probably disappear.

Here's another statistic for you to ponder. A bowling lane must be within 40/1,000ths of an inch in levelness and depth depression. There are rigid codes to see that a long list of specifications are met on every lane in every bowling center. Lanes are inspected regularly to insure their conformity, and certification can be withdrawn if the lanes are off in any way.

Since few bowlers ever have the opportunity to see a bowling pin up close, a few words might be of interest. Pins are generally made of wood with a plastic coating. Synthetic materials, including forms of magnesium, are also used; and different types of pins are being developed constantly.

An approved American Bowling Congress pin ranges in weight from 3 pounds, 2 ounces to 3 pounds, 10 ounces. The pin is 15 inches high with a base diameter of 2¼ inches and belly (fat part) diameter of 4¾ inches.

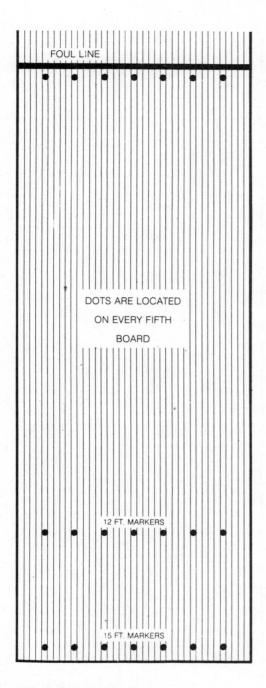

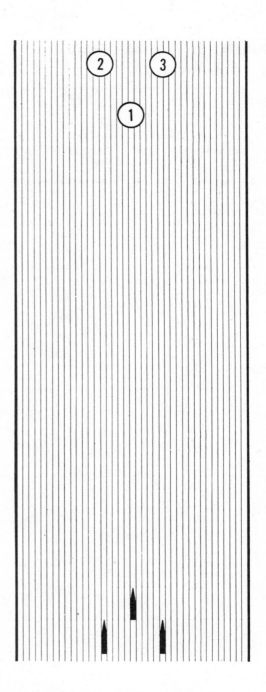

The Approach

The approach is 15 feet in length, with dots imbedded in the boards at the Foul Line, 12 feet behind the Foul Line, and sometimes 15 feet as well. These dots are helpful in determining your stance location and walk pattern. Some lanes have 7 dots at the 12 and 15 foot markers, but others have only 5 dots.

Arrows to the Pin Deck)

This 45 foot section of the lane is where the ball surface and lane surface interact to create the final portion of the path of the ball to the pins.

(From the Foul Line to the Arrows)

This 15 foot section of the lane has Arrows imbedded on every fifth board, and dots on boards 3, 5, 8, 11, and 14. These lane features can be of assistance in locating the proper line and angle for all lane conditions.

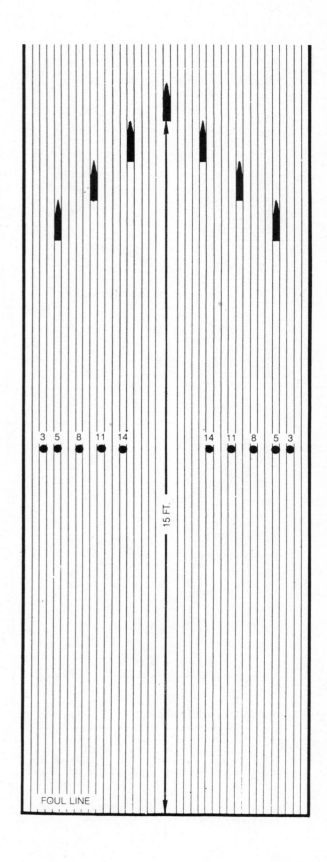

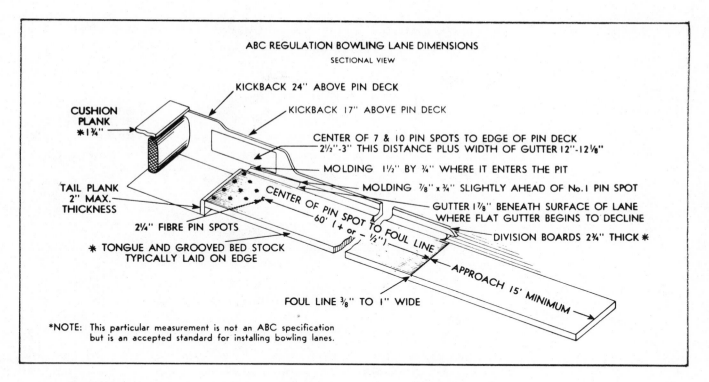

ABC REGULATION BOWLING LANE DIMENSIONS
SECTIONAL VIEW

KICKBACK 24" ABOVE PIN DECK

KICKBACK 17" ABOVE PIN DECK

CUSHION PLANK *1¾"

CENTER OF 7 & 10 PIN SPOTS TO EDGE OF PIN DECK 2½"-3" THIS DISTANCE PLUS WIDTH OF GUTTER 12"-12⅛"

MOLDING 1½" BY ¾" WHERE IT ENTERS THE PIT

MOLDING ⅞" x ¾" SLIGHTLY AHEAD OF No.1 PIN SPOT

TAIL PLANK 2" MAX. THICKNESS

CENTER OF PIN SPOT 60' (+ or - ½")

GUTTER 1⅞" BENEATH SURFACE OF LANE WHERE FLAT GUTTER BEGINS TO DECLINE

2¼" FIBRE PIN SPOTS

CENTER OF PIN SPOT TO FOUL LINE

DIVISION BOARDS 2¾" THICK *

* TONGUE AND GROOVED BED STOCK TYPICALLY LAID ON EDGE

APPROACH 15' MINIMUM

FOUL LINE ⅜" TO 1" WIDE

*NOTE: This particular measurement is not an ABC specification but is an accepted standard for installing bowling lanes.

Pins may seem small and helpless and close together when you're at the foul line. Don't you believe it. Those constant enemies make up a total of almost 40 pounds of tough wood and plastic, ready and able to repulse and deflect a bowling ball.

Bowling received its biggest push with the coming of the automatic pinspotter. AMF first unveiled its giant robots in 1946 and had them operating commercially in 1952. Brunswick soon followed, and now we take the amazing machines for granted. Pins had been set by human hands and drastically limited the size and hours of bowling centers. Now any bowling center can operate 24 hours a day.

Human foul judges were utilized to call fouls until electric eye automatic foul detectors came into use. And in recent years automatic scorers have become more and more popular. Computers are in use in one way or another in all bowling centers, from the control desk to the office, to check and record every phase of activity.

From the flick of a switch to turn on your lane, modern technology takes over; your ball rolls over the finest material money can buy, constructed by the best technicians. Your ball makes contact with pins that cost as much as ten dollars each. Then your ball goes into the cushion to trigger the mechanism of a machine that makes all ready for your second ball while sending your ball back through an efficient underground ball return system.

All this is for your enjoyment, so I urge you to always respect the

45

equipment in your bowling center; it's your home away from home, your private little country club, one that you could never afford but can control, just for the price of a game of bowling.

About Bowling Balls

The early bowling balls were made of wood, usually lignum vitae, so dense they wouldn't float in water. They were crude and after use lost their shape and balance. They were sent back to the early pro shops to be made round again but came back smaller each time.

The hard rubber ball came into its own shortly after the turn of the century; and from 1905 until 1960 when plastic bowling balls pioneered by Columbia Industries came on the scene, they dominated the sport. Later, combinations of rubber and plastic opened the doors to a whole new world of variety in color and composition.

A legal bowling ball, according to ABC and WIBC specifications, must be constructed of a nonmetallic composition without voids in its interior.

It cannot have a circumference of more than 27 inches; the diameter must be constant, and the weight limit of 16 pounds after drilling must conform to balance limits in top, bottom, and sides. No ball may have more than 3 ounces of top weight or 1 ounce of side or bottom weight. Bowling balls must also pass a hardness test and register no less than 72 on an instrument used to check hardness, called a *durometer*.

The span is the distance from the inside edge of the thumb hole

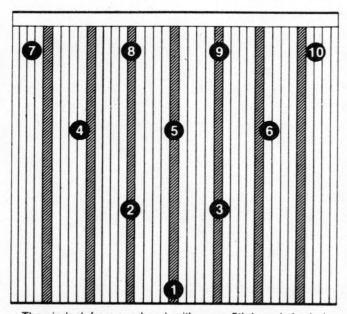

The pindeck from overhead, with every 5th board shaded.

to the inside edge of the finger holes.

Pitch is the angle at which the holes are drilled in relationship to the center of the ball.

The three basic bowling ball grips in bowling are the *conventional, fingertip,* and *semi-fingertip.*

In the conventional grip the thumb is placed all the way into the thumb hole. Then the two middle fingers are extended over the finger holes so that the bend of the second joint extends approximately ¼ inch beyond the inner edge of the finger holes.

The fingertip is drilled with a span so wide that the bowler can insert fingers only to the first joint or bend.

The semi-fingertip is a drilling that places the fingers in the holes somewhere between the conventional and fingertip.

There is no right or wrong grip: the conventional gives more feel of the ball, the fingertip is easier on the fingers and allows for more lift, and the semi-fingertip offers some of the advantages and disadvantages of both the others.

The Right Ball—for You

Let's get one thing straight. Practically anyone can bowl with any bowling ball. And some might even bowl well, but they pay with bad fingers, hands, wrists, or bowling faults caused by a ball.

And I speak from experience. I didn't know much about bowling balls and grips and fits when I first started; and though I bowled well, it cost me probably the best-known worst thumb in bowling history.

On the pindicator, numbers light up to indicate pins that are left standing.

47

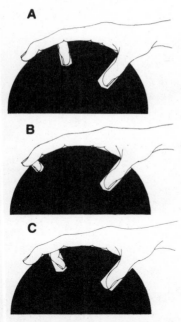

Three grips: A) conventional;
B) fingertip; C) semi-fingertip.

SPAN TOO WIDE

SPAN TOO NARROW

Once I settled in and got advice from my ball driller, Bob Simonelli, I overcame my problem.

Don't get me wrong. If you bowl too much, or not enough, you will get blisters and bruises and callus formations. After all, the only contact in the sport is your hand on the ball, and something has to give now and then and it's going to be your hand before the ball.

Let me tell you what I've learned about bowling balls. The right ball at the right time for a pro can mean a few extra pins a game, many thousands over a season, and maybe a couple of titles and many thousands of dollars. For you it can mean extra comfort, a league championship, or maybe a local title.

Bowlers often develop bad habits when they start out, and many of them are caused or accentuated by a poorly fitted ball or the use of a different ball every time they roll. The wrong ball can cause rushing, lagging, poor timing in every phase of the sport, dropping of the ball, hanging on to the ball, and a long list of other faults.

Bowling is a feel-and-finesse sport. As I mentioned, the main contact is your hand on the ball. I prefer a snug fit, and people always comment on how I seem to move my hand around before getting set. What I'm trying to do is to get the feel I want; I almost feel like I'm screwing my fingers and thumb into the ball to get the proper hold. And yet it isn't a clutch or a tense grab, it's a feeling of security, but in a relaxed way.

Some bowlers still use house balls, those supplied by the center. Forget that and buy your own ball. Then you know the same ball is available to you without any scrambling around, and you can't possibly hope to improve without owning your own ball.

How do you go about buying a bowling ball? Your bowling center is a good starting point. Many have pro shops operated by trained bowling ball specialists. If they don't, ask the owner or manager or check your local directory, but make sure you go to a pro. Don't try to save a few dollars by giving up the professional guidance. Any PBA member is a good bet.

Pros know and use only the best equipment because it means income to them. The bowling ball firms utilize the talents of the best engineers, chemists, and other craftsmen to produce quality balls. I have spent many hours at the Columbia plant, fascinated by what goes into the manufacturing of a bowling ball.

You might be dazzled by the vast amount of different-colored bowling balls, when years ago all bowling balls were black. Take your time and select the one you like, even if it's only because it matches your clothes, your car, or the color of your eyes.

The weight of the ball is important. I say simply use the maxi-

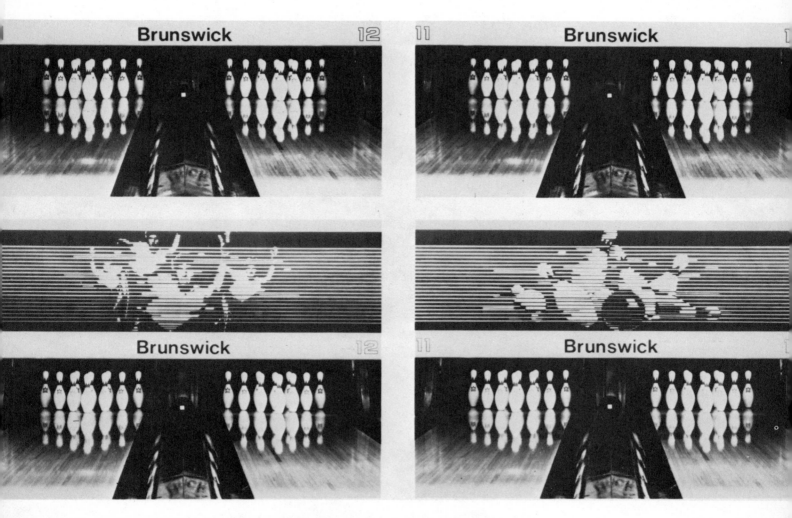

Just as personal equipment in bowling has come a long way, so have the color, design, and scenes the bowlers see when they step up to the line. A wide range of color-pleasing subjects either calm you or project you into a partial fantasy world before you roll the ball. Called masking units, they cover the complicated machinery that sets the pins and returns the ball back to the bowler at the approach area. Also incorporated into these dazzling displays are various indicators telling you whether it is your first or second ball, what pins you have left, and even ways to give you an idea on how to roll the pins that remain standing after the first ball is rolled.

49

Here Mark Roth shows
various finger spread
positions for the
fingers not inserted
into the finger holes.
This is an individual
choice, but the choice
is important because
these fingers can give
a better feel of the
ball and also help
to guide its direction.
Bowlers should test to
find what's best.
Opposite: Mark is
making sure that all
excess matter is
cleaned from the ball
so that his hand does
not stick or slide and
also to aid the ball
in rolling more con-
sistently.

mum weight at which you can comfortably handle the ball. Most men, and many women, can easily handle the 16-pounders. And it's not a matter of strength. I've seen 100-pound women toss a 16-pounder with ease because they have the proper bowling ball fit and balance. Most women should be in the 14- to 15-pound range and youngsters from 8 pounds up.

Test the various weights before you decide. Swing the ball while taking your normal approach. If it sways or drags your hand, arm or shoulder, forcing them down too quickly, then go to a lighter weight. I would always advise lighter weights for older bowlers and those with any sort of physical disability.

Whatever pin-carrying power you might lose with a lighter ball is more than made up for in comfort and ability to handle and control the ball properly.

Fitting a bowling ball is an art. No two hands are the same. Fingers are long and slender, short and puffy, and the skin and muscles of a hand range from great elasticity to almost rigid firmness. All this, plus personality and other physical characteristics, must be taken into account.

The main object is to have a ball that will enable you to get to the line and release it smoothly so that you will attain consistency. A personally fitted ball that feels just about the same every time gives you a good start.

A word of caution. If you have been using a house ball or one given to you by a relative or friend, odds are the holes have been much too large; and because you got used to that, your own personal ball might feel snug, even tight. Don't worry about it; you should get used to it in a short time.

What about the grip? It is vital that the person drilling your ball take the time to closely examine your hand, check you physically, learn a little about how you get to the line and how you release a ball. The more he knows about you, the more clues he has to give you the grip you need.

All factors applying to beginning bowlers hold true for the intermediate and experts, too; but there is a big difference in fitting them for a bowling ball. The better bowler has achieved a certain amount of consistency. He gets to the line about the same way each time, and he either hooks a ball or he doesn't. When he goes to an additional ball, he should be looking for a ball to give him another weapon. And he can do it even with essentially the same grip.

This bowler can move into the worlds of balance and hardness because there is a vast spectrum of bowling ball versatility within the legal scope.

A bowling ball, before it is drilled, has a *weight block,* the area in which the ball is drilled. However, it can be drilled so that there is positive weight, negative weight, thumb, finger, top, bottom, and side weights. Any single weight or balance factor can produce changes in how the ball will roll and how effective it will be.

With combinations of weight factors, the variations are endless. Add to that the fact that balls can be of varying hardness and you can see that bowling balls are of infinite variety. Few bowlers have the knowledge and experience to put these factors to practical use, and that's why you should always go to an expert.

However, you do have eyesight and common sense. Watch your ball as it goes down the lane, how it hits, how it acts and reacts. Do you want or need more hook? Less hook? Then drillings and ball surface can help you. If you want more skid and less hook, go to a harder surface ball. If you want more hook, the softer surface ball will grab better and give you more of a break.

I tend to agree with early pro and Hall-of-Famer Vince Lucci, who when asked about the difference between bowling in his day and now, commented, ''In my day, if you had trouble, you moved on the approach, changed your angle or speed, and had to concentrate on what move was the right one. These days, if you know what you're doing, much of that can be accomplished just by changing your bowling ball.''

I think every serious bowler should have a minimum of two bowling balls, to be able to make these changes. It's better to change your bowling ball to adapt to a lane condition than change your style. The results with the right extra ball are quicker and better. That way you can still use the area on the lane where you prefer to bowl and are most comfortable.

Prior to a pro tournament block, we receive four practice balls on each lane. It's then I make my decision of what ball to use. Most of the grips are the same, but each is a little different in balance and hardness.

Former PBA national champ Bob Strampe once joked, ''If they could carry them, pro bowlers would have a different ball for each lane.'' I don't suggest anything so drastic, but I do urge you to be flexible.''

I can best illustrate that with a story about Tom Hudson, one of our top pros and a guy we all look up to in the matter of bowling ball knowledge.

In the 1977 AMF Grand Prix he rolled a 300 game alternating bowling balls. In practice he felt the right lane reacted better to a rubber ball and the left better to a plastic ball. So that's just what he did for one of the most unique perfect games in bowling history, and a perfect example of what a bowling ball, properly used, can do.

I urge every bowler, even the most casual, to make every effort to have a personal bowling ball. But there are times when your ball might not be available or you might have a friend or relative along who doesn't own a ball.

Each center supplies what they call house balls for use by the customers. Here's what to look for if you must use a house ball. Find a suitable weight by swinging with a few of varying weights. Then place your thumb into the thumb hole all the way. Turn your thumb around back and forth. There should be just enough friction to allow you the feel of the ball.

With your thumb in the ball, stretch your fingers over the circumference of the ball until the second joint of the middle finger extends about a quarter of an inch beyond the inner edge of the finger hole. The fingers should feel snug but not so that you are locked into the holes in any manner. You will be able to use a house ball without too much trouble, but it will never match a ball fitted to your hand.

Safety

Bowling can hardly be considered a dangerous sport, but don't tell that to anyone who has had a finger or hand caught between two bowling balls or is nursing a sore toe or foot, the victim of a dropped bowling ball.

Always use two hands to pick up your ball from the ball-return rack. Place your hands on the two outer sides of the ball, away from where the other returning balls make contact.

Don't put your fingers in the holes when you pick up your ball. One reason is that you don't want to get them caught. Another is that placing the fingers in the ball while the ball is still on the rack can often give you the wrong feel of the ball and possibly cause sticking or slipping.

Never interfere with bowling center equipment or attempt to correct any malfunction. Never stick your hands or fingers into the ball return or attempt to retrieve stuck bowling balls in the underground return area. And don't ever go down the lane to clear any wayward pins or go near the pin-spotting machines.

Every center has some form of communication from the lanes to the desk, and it's a simple matter for the trained personnel to take care of any problem.

Bowling Bags

There's been a revolution in bowling bags. Once the bowling bag was

54

55

designed to carry a single bowling ball, was made of burlap or canvas, and didn't even have enough room for a pair of shoes.

Now the rage is compact two-ball bowling bags, with plenty of room for shoes, towels, and all the rest. Pros buy two-balled bags to carry two bowling balls. Many bowlers buy two-balled bags to carry one ball and all the rest, including knitting or books to read between frames of a dull game.

In all seriousness, bowling bags take plenty of abuse. They are tossed into the trunk of the car, dragged out, and tossed back in over and over again except when they're relegated to the cellar or the attic. Bowling bags come in various materials, from the most expensive leather to the cheapest cloths, and all the fine plastics and synthetics in between the two.

Make sure your bowling bag is well constructed, particularly the handle, which takes the most strain; and make sure there is plenty of room for the shoes so you don't have to force them all out of shape to get them in the bag. You have an investment in your ball, shoes, and other equipment. The bag protects it all; so whether you go for a single ball bag, a double ball, one of the chic suitcase styles, or one of the futuristic hard plastic models, select one with care.

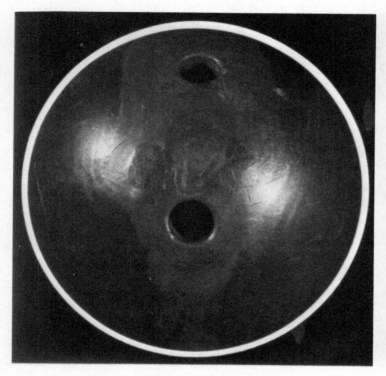

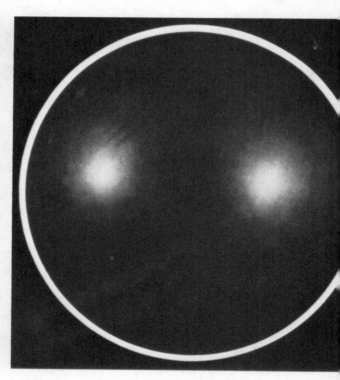

19th Century Wooden Ball   **Rubber Ball**

Bob Strampe, pictured with his trusty bowling ball, is a wit as well as a champion. He once noted that if bowlers could carry them, they would have a different ball for every lane. And he wasn't far from wrong. Pros may carry dozens of bowling balls in their motor homes or cars, and in competition may use as many as half a dozen in a single event or even a single day. A bowling ball is a weapon, to be chosen and cherished. Deep research goes into every new bowling ball. A new ball is a source of new inspiration to any bowler, so it gives mental as well as physical help. Every bowler also has the age-old dilemma of how to part with an old friend, the old bowling ball. The answer is simple, just keep it. Many bowling balls more than 50 years old are still in use. Nobody ever seems to throw them away, yet every bowler always wants to keep up-to-date with the new models, too. As a bowler, you can live with both, and make good use of both the old and the new.

Columbia Yellow Dot

Bowling Shoes

I can never quite figure out why so many people keep renting bowling shoes. What they spend for renting could better be used toward buying their own shoes.

I think it was Carmen Salvino, one of our most colorful pros, who told a group at a clinic, "If you want to forget all your other troubles, just try to bowl in a tight-fitting pair of bowling shoes."

He is so right. Bowling shoes must be snug, but they must be comfortable. It's true, according to scientific studies at the New York College of Podiatric Medicine, that most people have one foot about a half-size bigger than the other. The left foot is bigger in righties and the right foot larger in lefties.

Too often there isn't enough selection in bowling shoes, and people look for the wrong things—color, style, price. A properly executed delivery ends in a slide; and, therefore, the shoes that are specially constructed to allow a bowler both gripping and sliding freedom by the use of different materials on the soles of each shoe are still the best. The better shoes will have a leather tip on the nonsliding shoe for even greater wear and protection.

Some shoes are stitched, some glued. Bowling shoes take plenty of abuse, so it pays to get the best. There are custom-made shoes available that guarantee you a perfect fit and, with proper care, can last almost a normal bowling lifetime. Also, the heels and other parts of a shoe can wear down, and if the shoes are well made, a shoemaker will be able to repair them. Good footwork can often start with a good pair of bowling shoes.

Clothing

Avoid extremes in clothing. Be comfortable. Loose clothing is best but not so large that flowing skirts, blouses or shirts get in the way of arm and leg movement. Don't overlook the underclothes to give support as needed. And a most important part of clothing gear is the socks. Because you give your feet a pounding, I suggest good heavy socks, the kind that can absorb any perspiration and at the same time give you a good cushion.

Bowling shirts are available in all colors, materials, and styles. One of the fabled parts of bowling lore is the beautiful embroidery on the back. In many leagues the shirt may advertise a local tavern, restaurant, or anything else. I once saw a shirt advertising an undertaker, and on the back was a casket, complete with a body in it.

Dale Glenn, one of our pro bowlers from California, is nicknamed the Eagle, and for good reason; he often gives an eaglelike scream when he comes up with a big game or win. Glenn had one of his shirts embroidered with the most beautiful eagle ever conceived. Another pro, Larry Laub, took one look at it and quipped, "Dale is the only guy I know who advertises the United States on his shirt."

Bowling Aids or Accessories

It's often been said that for every bowler there's at least two instructors. Sometimes I think there is a bowling aid for every possible problem. In my time in bowling I've seen all kinds of inserts for the fingers and thumbs of bowling balls to give you better feel, more lift, less friction, and many other promises.

Then there are various types of gloves and wrist supports, grip aids in cream or powder form, sliding helps, all types of patching equipment to cover or soothe hurts, and even such things as weight balancers to be worn on wrists or ankles, shoulder straps to keep your arm close, and, yes, blinders.

Some of these things are great and really work. Others are practically worthless. I think every bowler should have what I call an emergency grab bag. In it should be tape, scissors, cotton, some sandpaper or other abrasive, the wrist band or gloves of your choice, a small manicuring kit, a knife, and whatever your favorite accessory might be.

Don't be afraid to try any bowling aid. If it helps you even a little, then it's worth the price. Don't expect too much and you won't be disappointed. If an aid doesn't help you, discard it.

FRAME

4

TO THE LINE

I still laugh when I see repeats of the old Jackie Gleason shows. In one episode Gleason and Art Carney are playing golf and Gleason tells newcomer-to-the-sport Carney to address the ball. Carney looks down and says, "Hello, ball."

It's a funny scene, but in reality I know more than a few bowlers who talk to their bowling balls or themselves or both. It's a form of concentration, a way to relax and check what must be checked before the most important phase of good bowling, getting to the line.

Let's begin with the starting position. You can arrive at the best stance by logical experimentation, based on how many steps you take, the size of your steps, and what is most comfortable for you.

For instance, if you use the four-step delivery, the one best for most bowlers, stand at the foul line, facing away from the pin area. Take the same type of step you would if you had a bowling ball in your hand headed for the pins. Take four steps, add another half step for a slide reserve, then do an about-face and look at the floor.

Check out the dots on the approach. Take a few practice strides down the approach. When you are satisfied that you have found what suits you best, mentally mark the exact spot you want to place the toe of the foot you want to use as your guide (usually the left in a four-step delivery).

Your steps from the foul line will give you your starting point lengthwise. In relation to the width of the lane, you should be to the right of the center dot, positioned so that your arm swing will roll the ball over a target area from the second to third arrow, the 10th to the 15th boards starting from the right.

Now you have your point of origin. This can be changed whenever you change the number of steps you take or the size of the steps. Our discussions are pointed at right-handed bowlers. The reverse is true for left-handers.

Stance or Address

After you have determined your starting point, give some close attention to your stance. You should be as relaxed as possible, but not so loose that you don't have control of every part of your body. A deep breath often helps.

The weight of the ball is supported by the nonbowling hand. The position of the ball in relation to the body can vary according to body structure, but avoid extremes of too high or too low, above the shoulders or below the knees. Ideally, any position between the waist and

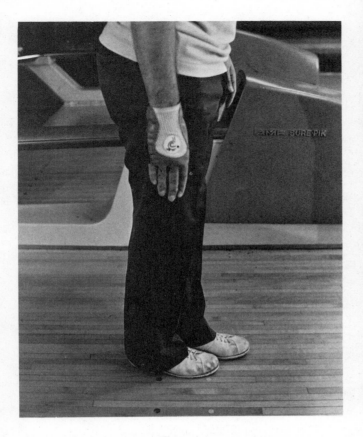

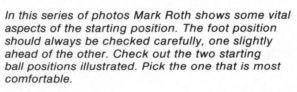

In this series of photos Mark Roth shows some vital aspects of the starting position. The foot position should always be checked carefully, one slightly ahead of the other. Check out the two starting ball positions illustrated. Pick the one that is most comfortable.

HOW TO AVOID
RUSHING THE LINE

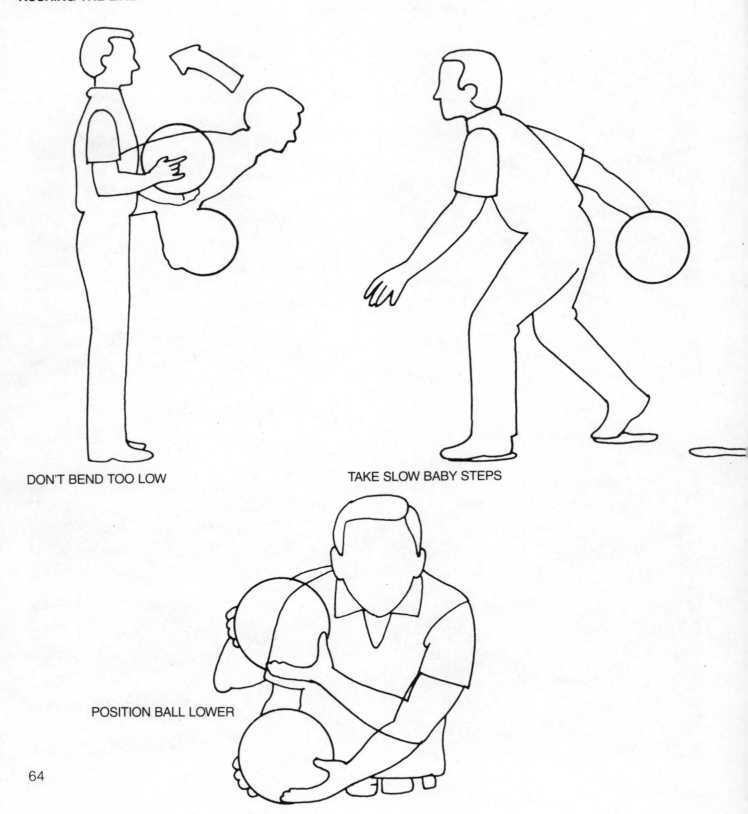

DON'T BEND TOO LOW

TAKE SLOW BABY STEPS

POSITION BALL LOWER

top of the shoulder is within the best range.

Hold the ball to the right of the body to give you a good start on a straight arm swing. That's where you want the ball to swing from so it makes it easier to start there than to bring the ball from the center of the body or elsewhere.

Don't Hold Tight

Many bowlers are fully relaxed in their starting position and grip the ball in an ideal manner. But once they begin their approach, they squeeze and tighten the grip, almost clutching for dear life. This prevents a proper release and can be very tiring.

The first part of the arm swing should bring no great change in the gripping action. As the ball is brought to the final release point, there is a natural tendency to tighten up as you attempt to apply some extra lift.

Accept a little extra gripping, but don't fear that you will lose anything if you don't. You can always apply better action to the ball if at your final release point the ball is held firmly rather than clutched.

Think smooth, think reach, think target and that will help you forget to think tighter grip.

Keep your bowling arm close to your body. Your wrist should be fairly straight and firm, and fingers should be well in the ball with the thumb inserted all the way. The thumb should be at approximately 11 o'clock if you look at the ball as the face of a clock.

Shoulders are best when squared or parallel to your target, and your eyes should be intent on the target, the second arrow or 10th board area mentioned previously.

Keep your feet fairly close together, with the left foot slightly extended and the big toe straight, even with the boards toward the pins. Most of the weight should be on the left foot, and the knees should not be stiff but slightly flexed.

The purpose of the stance is to position yourself so that with the least amount of effort and very little thinking, you can begin your approach without strain and continue in a smooth delivery from launch to ball release.

Pushaway, Arm Swing, Steps

The *pushaway* is the movement of the ball and starting foot together to begin the approach. The ball should be pushed straight ahead, and the starting foot, the right foot, goes forward at the same time. Don't try to push the ball up or down because any jerky motions or off-balance movements will be magnified by the time you reach the foul line.

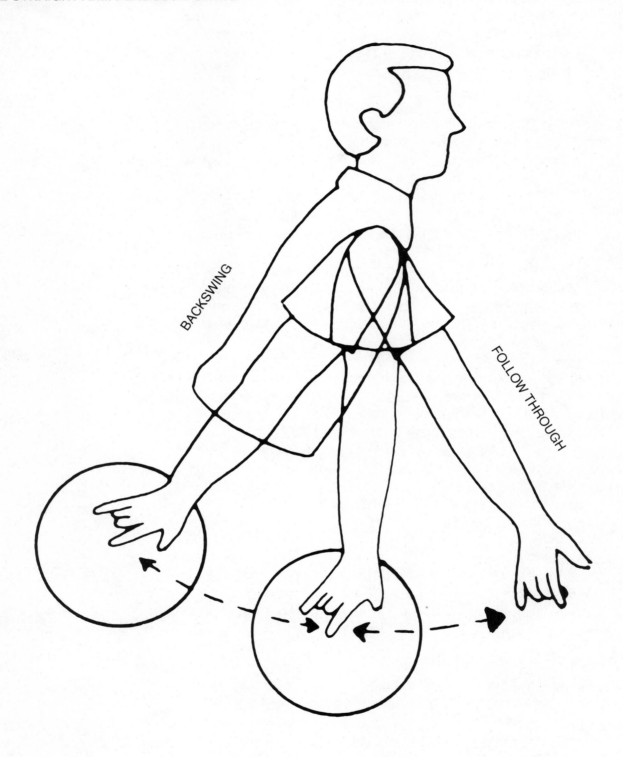

BACKSWING

FOLLOW THROUGH

TOP VIEW OF STRAIGHT ARM PENDULUM SWING

BACKSWING FOLLOW THROUGH

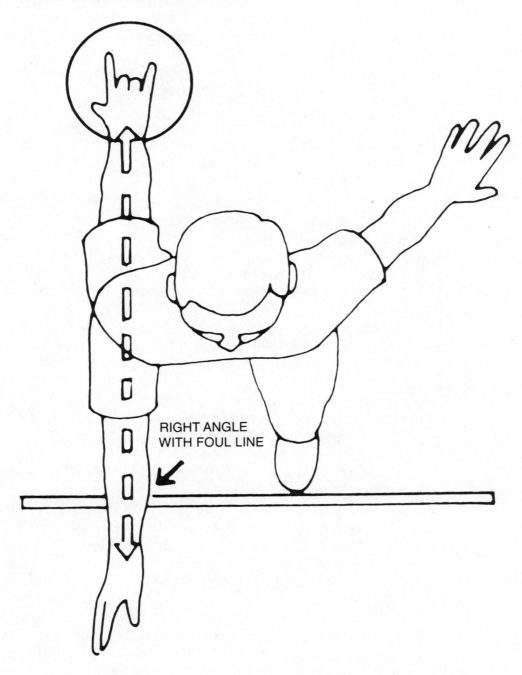

RIGHT ANGLE
WITH FOUL LINE

Rushing is the number-one problem of all bowlers, because there's a natural tendency to want to get going, an eagerness to kill the pins. If you get the ball out straight in the pushaway, it will drop at the end to create a good natural swing without any extra help, so don't drive the ball down.

Take it as slow as possible on that first step, and the second one, too; but don't let it bother you if you are a little swift. You can't be a robot.

Four steps is the distance most bowlers should take and the approach most experts recommend, and for good reason. Three steps tend to make you too fast, get the ball into motion too quickly, and require too much strength to be consistent. The three-step delivery is quick all the way, and the first step must incorporate the first two steps of the four-step style, thus demanding a more definite downward and more rapid pushaway.

The five-step is basically the same as the four-step, accomplished by adding another step in the beginning in which the ball is held practically stationary. Thus, the second step of the five-step delivery is much the same as the first step in the four-step delivery. Five steps are fine if you feel the need for a longer approach for any good reason— long legs, way to generate more speed or momentum, or just plain comfort.

But let's look at the four-step in more detail. At the end of the first step or pushaway, your waist and knees should be bending slightly and your nonbowling hand is still carrying much of the weight of the ball.

When you get into the second step, the nonbowling hand leaves the ball and the bowling arm and ball go into the free pendulum swing. Little help is needed from the bowler as the weight of the ball will do the job, much as the pendulum of a clock or an object suspended by chain from a height where the weight of the object gives the needed initial impetus.

Your left arm will move out and seek the best level to give you added balance. Your right arm should still be close to your body, and though the second step may be a bit longer than the first, it should still be on the short side.

At the completion of the second step the shoulders are square to the target, the left foot is forward, and the ball is below the shoulder.

If the arm swing never goes higher than the shoulder, the odds are you are in great balance and control. Too high can cause you all sorts of problems, so don't try to force the swing up and away. On the lower side of a swing, the waist should be the low limit. But you need go back only as far as you must to maintain decent speed on the ball.

In this sequence Roth displays his power-packed delivery from start to finish. He is always firm but relaxed, despite his speed to the line and his back swing, one of the highest of any star bowler. He maintains his balance; the timing of his arm and leg swing is amazing, even at the peak of his high arm swing. His feet are just where he wants them in order to impart his final lift and turn, the result being an action ball.

Bowling technique has a split-second moment of truth
that can make or break any single given release of the
ball. Note here in Roth's finishing step how he
is firmly planted with the left foot at the line as
his arm is coming forward to bring the ball across
the foul line. His left foot is straight, and his
right foot is off the floor to give him more balance.
You can almost feel the power he is generating
as he applies his famous lift to the ball at the
last moment. He is solidly planted in every way.

The ball reaches the peak of the back swing when the third step is completed. At that point the right foot is well forward, left arm extended and body still square to the target.

The weight is still on the right foot at the beginning of the fourth and final step; but then it shifts to the left foot, which enters into a slide. The right foot and leg are then released to either brake a bowler by dragging on the floor or by remaining aloft to help achieve better balance.

Timing is considered perfect when your left foot and right arm reach the foul line at just about the same time, the slide has been completed, and the ball release is starting. The left foot is firmly planted at the line with the weight concentrated on the front of the left foot. A good left knee bend and a body low at the finish are great aids in gaining the best leverage.

You can be a creature of your environment, even in bowling style. There was a national team tournament that proved this conclusively. All the attention was on a team from a very small town in the Midwest, not because they were rolling so well but because of their peculiar approach to the line. Each man would take two perfectly normal steps, then all of a sudden would dip down low for a step and then come back up a bit.

When asked if they all learned from the same teacher, the captain smiled, "No, we roll in a tiny bowling center in the basement of an old building where space was cramped. There's plenty of space up for the first two steps, but if we don't adopt that dip on the third step, we'll just bang our heads on the pipes hanging down in the third-step area."

Mark Roth shows the start of the four-step delivery as it should be performed. The first two steps should be short and somewhat relaxed, getting you in motion.

73

Roth continues with the four-step at the top of the backswing and into the final slide. The camera catches him just as he releases the ball with follow-through.

75

This is the sight most of Mark Roth's opponents see from the bench as he delivers his ball. In Roth's release the left foot is slightly turned for him to regain balance after his rush to the line, right foot is up and away for extra leverage as is the left arm for better balance.

These unique behind-the-foul-line pictures show Mark Roth's approach from a different angle. Roth is a strong bowler with plenty of power in his arms, legs, and body, and this is shown in the manner in which he easily carries and controls his 16-pound bowling ball. Note how his body moves just enough to allow the arm swing to clear, though he still maintains his almost straight approach to the line or to his target.

FRAME
5

TO THE TARGET

All your preparation, from the fitting of your equipment to the development of a good stance and approach, are designed to lead up to one thing, proper ball release.

That exact split second when you let the ball go determines what the ball will do once it starts down the lane. And you control the ball. Once again envision the bowling ball as a clock. In bowling you basically have a straight ball, hook, curve, and reverse hook or backup. Your thumb position at the point of ball release in relation to your imaginary clock will determine what the ball will do.

If your thumb placement at point of release is 12 o'clock, directed straight forward towards the target, the ball will roll straight.

The hook ball is preferred by most better bowlers. A thumb position of 10 to 11 o'clock at the point of ball release will produce a hook ball.

The curve ball is produced the same way as a hook, but the thumb direction position is lower than 10 o'clock, and additional lift is given at point of release.

The reverse hook, or backup, is the result of clockwise revolutions, as contrasted to the counterclockwise revolving motions of the hook ball; and it is the result of a ball release with the thumb at 1 to 2 o'clock.

What happens at the point of release? The thumb exits the ball first, leaving the ball resting and supported on the flats of the fingers for a split second. You can actually feel this if you concentrate, and it's one of the feels a bowler must look for all the time.

It is at this precise point that the so-called lift is applied. The lift is the feel of the flats of the fingers on the inside of the finger holes. Thumb positions plus lift at the point of ball release determine the revolutions imparted to the ball, which in turn creates or causes a slight or large hook, curve, or backup.

There is no great mystery to hooking a ball. Practice the proper positioning of thumb and fingers. If you wish to gain the proper feel of lifting a ball, place your fingers in the ball but don't insert the thumb. Then roll the ball. You will be forced to press the flats of the fingers against the holes of the ball in order to roll it. That's the feel you're looking for at ball release.

It would be fine if you could say that these basic facts are constant. They are not. Lane conditions also play a major role. Lanes are cleaned and coated with oils and dressings and compounds to protect the wood in many different ways. Excessive dressing will lessen the

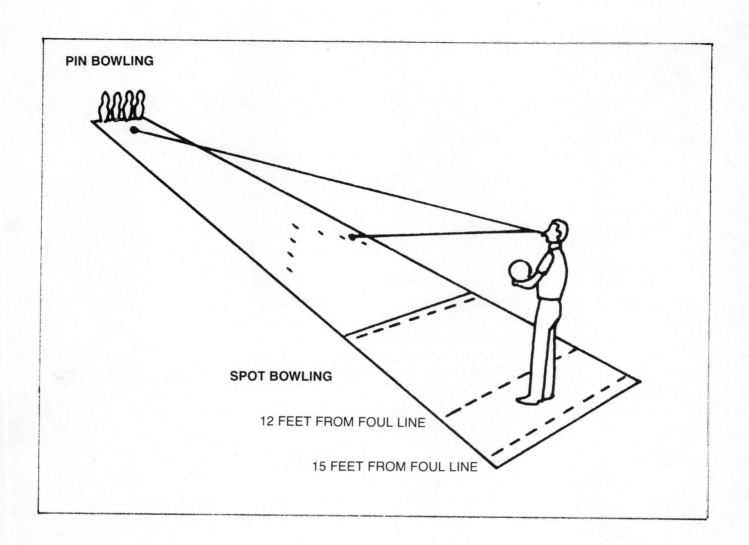

PIN BOWLING

SPOT BOWLING

12 FEET FROM FOUL LINE

15 FEET FROM FOUL LINE

82

friction and retard the grabbing and hooking action, causing the ball to slide. Minimal dressing or lanes that have had many games rolled on them will allow the ball to hook easier because there is more friction. A few practice shots or a few balls and trial-and-error should quickly tell you whether lanes are hooking or not.

When softer-surfaced bowling balls were introduced, bowlers found they could easily alter the size of the hook by changing from one ball to another. Fine, but many bowlers own only a single ball, and even those that own more than one don't always have the extra ones available.

So remember, you can always move toward the center of the lane to cut down the hook or to the outside to increase the hook. Your hand release can also help.

As noted, the basic hand release has the thumb in the 10- to 11-o'clock direction, wrist firm, and fingers lifting as though you were trying to go through the ball with an upward motion. If you want a little extra hook to compensate for a nonhooking lane surface, cup your wrist a bit and that will force you to apply extra lift, producing more break, with little extra effort on your part.

I cup and really turn my wrist, and that makes my ball skid longer and hook sharper at the end when the revolutions start churning.

When you want less hook, you can use a weaker wrist action during the release, imparting less lift, or just try to impart less lift. This can be dangerous. I always feel you should put as much as you can on the ball; and once you learn that, don't go backwards. There are all types of variations on ball release. Experiment with them to find what is best for you most of the time and what you can switch to as an alternate if things aren't going just right.

The ball should be released on the up-swing as you begin the upper arc of your swing, not at any point during the down-swing. All too often you hear about throwing a bowling ball. A bowling ball should be rolled. It should be tossed out on the lane at least a foot or more, but much like a plane landing, not lofting it up so that it hits with a thud and almost leaves a ball crater on the lane.

At the completion of the final step of your delivery, your left knee is bent, you are in good balance, and your right arm is smoothly lifting the ball well over the foul line; and as you release the ball you move right into your follow-through.

There's a school of thought that says follow-through means absolutely nothing since the ball is already gone, and you can't do much once the ball is out of your hand. I don't buy that. To me the follow-through is not a different or separate part of the delivery but an important part of the overall package.

These simple charts graphically show the line of the straight, hook, and curve ball, and the approximate place to stand on the approach. Always understand that there is no such thing as a true straight ball and that each bowler must adjust for the type of ball that he typically rolls on a normal lane condition.

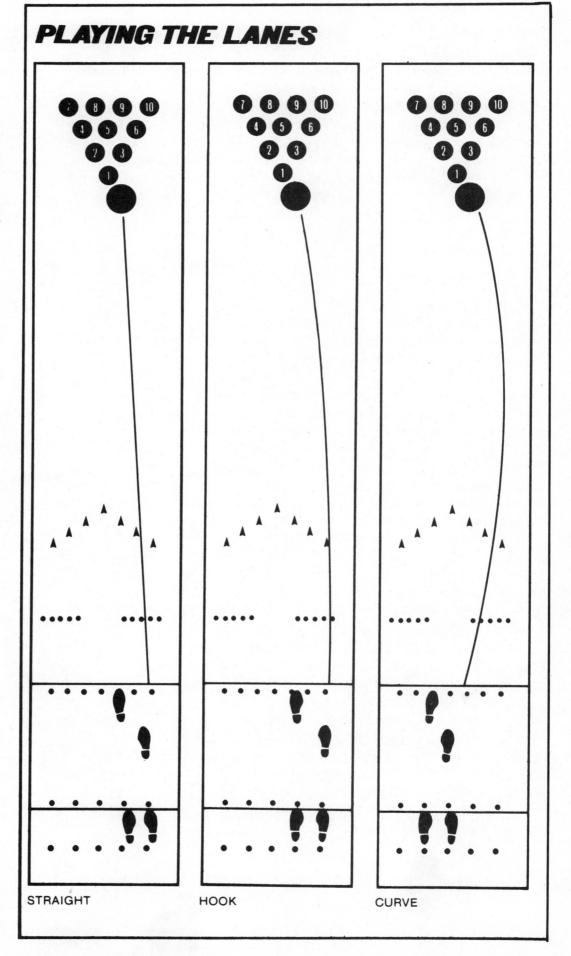

PLAYING THE LANES

STRAIGHT

HOOK

CURVE

84

You should always be reaching towards your target, and the follow-through will help you direct your arm and shoulder to the target area, forcing you to get into the shot, a phrase you hear often in bowling.

The follow-through is a continuation of the natural arc of the swing that started way back there with the pushaway. Follow-through is usually considered useless or the part of your game that gets the blame for faults that can't be explained in other ways. Your follow-through must be considered an important part of your game, not just a fancy show at the end of the delivery and ball release. Its worth—in forcing you to extend, to get a better line on your target, and making your delivery complete—cannot be denied.

Once your ball has been released, you are not free from responsibility. Follow the course of the ball carefully. Watch where it rolls, how it rolls, and note how close you came to your target and, if you missed it, on which side and by how much. Store all that information, but not for long, because it should help you to determine what changes, if any, you must make on the next shot.

A word here about ball release in regard to the obvious fear some people show, scared stiff that the ball won't let go. Such thoughts are often reinforced by silly skits on TV situation comedies when a bowling ball always gets stuck to a finger, thumb, or even a toe.

When fitted properly and released the way it should be, a bowling ball won't stick to your thumb because it can't. All that force and pressure coming down won't permit you to hang on. However, if there is a great change in the weather and your hand swells, or you roll too many games, or get some foreign matter caught in the hole, or tense up and clutch the ball, it could hang up on you. Just relax, make sure the hole is clean, and it should never happen to you.

I do remember, though, that in a tournament at Madison Square Garden Palmer Fallgren, one of the strongest men on tour, picked up his ball a little too quickly, didn't insert his hand properly, and the thumb hung and the ball went flying up, and up, until it hit the ceiling. It was the first and last time I ever saw anything like that happen, except in the movies.

Ball Track

The *bowling ball track* is the area where the ball makes contact with the lane while rolling; and it's easy to find because the tiny portion, just a fraction of an inch, making contact with the lane picks up minute particles of dust and lane finish.

To determine the type of ball you roll, picture your ball as a sphere. If the track or mark goes around the full circumference of the ball, between the thumb and fingers, it's a *full roller.* If it shows on about three-quarters of the circumference, anywhere up to some 2 inches left of the thumb, it's known as a *semi-roller.* If there's a circle to the left of the thumb hole, and it could vary in size, then your ball is of the *spinner* variety.

These days the semi-roller is the most effective type ball and the spinner the least. Over the years all three have been used by some of the biggest names. The roll of your ball is the result of the way you deliver the ball and the type of action you impart. Your roll is natural for you, and unless you need a drastic change, don't worry about it. Many top bowlers have had problems when trying to switch their roll.

It's helpful to know the ball track should you decide to buy a new ball; then the ball fitter and driller can reinforce your strong points by the use of allowable weight tolerances.

Ball Revolutions

The number of times a ball revolves going down the lane seems to interest people. I'm told this number varies greatly, with 9 to 13 being acceptable. I get as many as 16, I'm told. I never really counted them and don't worry too much. I know I get the ball working better by giving it more lift. I like to get it well down the lane, let it skid and slide a bit, and then start turning over.

When the ball breaks and the revolutions take hold, the ball actually speeds up into the pocket and mixes the pins much better.

When I want to skid more, I don't lift as much and turn my hand off to the right a bit.

ROLLERS

FULL
CIRCUMFERENCE

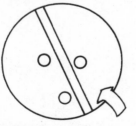

GENERALLY BETWEEN
FINGER HOLES

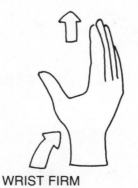

WRIST FIRM

SEMI OR
THREE-QUARTER

GENERALLY BELOW
THUMB HOLE

WRIST SLIGHTLY
BROKEN

SPINNER

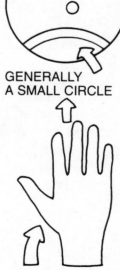

GENERALLY
A SMALL CIRCLE

HAND ON TOP
OF BALL

CLOCKING YOUR HOOK

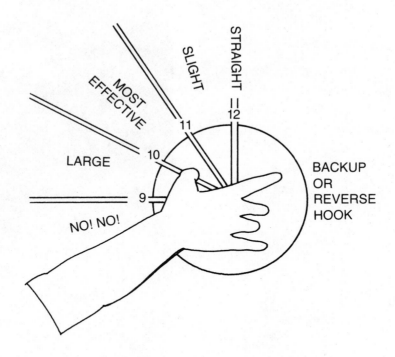

MOST
EFFECTIVE

SLIGHT

STRAIGHT

11

12

10

LARGE

9

NO! NO!

BACKUP
OR
REVERSE
HOOK

AT BALL RELEASE

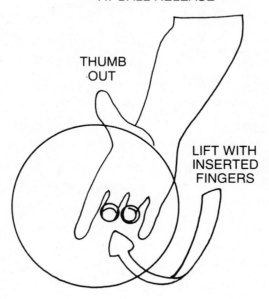

THUMB
OUT

LIFT WITH
INSERTED
FINGERS

In these two photos Mark Roth displays his high swing. This is not recommended for any bowler unless it is completely natural as it is with Roth. He himself was not aware of how high his swing was until he began to study his own game on video tape. In his case it works well; it gives him extra speed when he needs it. Any bowler attempting to develop such a high swing would probably ruin his timing. Opposite: Front view of hand position for a straight ball.

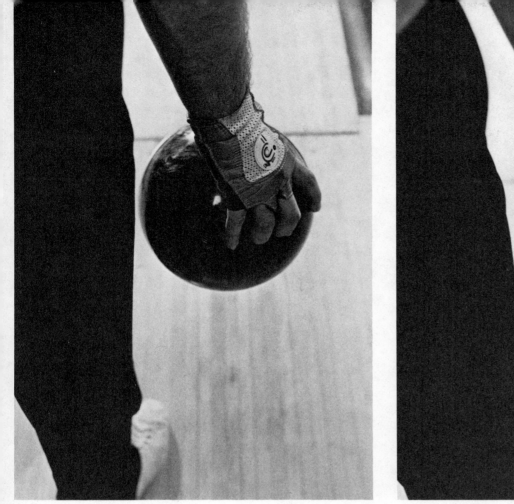

So that the reader can gain a better idea of the finger and thumb positions necessary to roll the straight ball, Mark Roth posed these closeup shots. Note that when the thumb is straight forward the ball will roll straight, when it is to the left the ball will revolve left, and cause the hooking action desired to execute the hook and curve ball as described in the text.

Here is the moment of truth in bowling, that split second when the thumb has left the ball and it rests on the fingers. Study the pictures on this and the next page to see how you can gain the feel needed for the proper ball release. It is at this point that the action is imparted to the ball.

FRAME
6

THE TARGET

As previously mentioned, the series of dots on the approach and the arrowlike markings in the lane are there to help guide you to your target, the 1–3 pocket, with a minimum of difficulty.

Practically all pros are spot or line bowlers, yet many beginners and amateurs are what is known as *pin bowlers.* A pin bowler keeps his eyes on the 1–3 pocket and tries to hit the target the best way he can without any real battle plan.

It is certainly much easier to hit a spot that is 3, 6, 12, or 15 feet away than it is to hit a target 60 feet away, and that's the simple logic behind spot bowling. The target arrow on a lane or certain board serves as your guide. If your approach, angle, and ball speed are about the same each roll and you hit your spot, then you will make contact with the 1–3 strike pocket.

There are few limitations on spot bowling. It isn't necessary to select a spot as far out on the lane as the arrows. If you prefer a closer spot, check the line to the arrow and pick any distinguishing characteristic along the line. Some bowlers spot just at or slightly beyond the foul line.

Line bowling could be classed as a combination of spot and pin bowling and rates as a popular form of targeting. The idea is to draw an imaginary line along your ball path, from the time the ball is released until the time it hits the pins. Then select a couple of specific points along that line, the point being that if you hit those two points along the line you have set up, your ball will hit the final target. There are many variations of line bowling, all based on what type of target is easiest for you to hit.

Area bowling is simply giving yourself a larger area to hit. Instead of selecting a single board or arrow, you settle for a general area around that specific target, giving yourself a larger margin of error. That's the method I prefer because it tends to loosen a bowler from the pressure of hitting a tiny target. When you feel you have a larger target, you usually pinpoint much better.

You often hear about pros being able to hit a dime anywhere on the lane. It's true. When I practiced, that's just what I used to do, place a dime as my target and keep practicing until I could hit it 49 times out of 50.

I also placed little strips of tape on the lane and practiced endless hours on hitting the strips of tape from various angles. You may feel that a bowling center won't allow you to do such things, but most of them will if you explain that you want to practice and are careful not to damage or mark up the lanes in any way.

I can't repeat enough that all targeting systems depend on consistency. Any changes in starting and finishing positions, any change in angle and speed, and any change in ball delivery will result in the ball hitting differently even though you manage to make contact with the desired target on the lane.

A targeting system in which you have confidence is the key, whether you spot at the foul line or a few feet before the pins. The best bowlers have discovered that some form of spot, line, or area bowling gives you the best results, so try to find your specific method in the general area most comfortable to you, whether it be first or fourth arrow.

Instinct

I have been told that there is no such thing as instinct. I have also been told that I'm one of the great instinct bowlers of all time.

Maybe that's the wrong word, instinct; maybe it should be called an awareness of something going wrong that must be changed in order to avoid disaster, in this case, a bad shot. I normally take six steps in my approach, yet I have been known to take seven or eight, and at times I did it without even knowing. All I knew was that my body just didn't feel right and so I added a step or two. Honestly, I really didn't even have to think about it. If you put your hand on a hot stove or too close to a match, you move it away quickly. That's the way I feel about instinct—it just happens.

It happens when you're at the line and you know that somewhere along the way you just didn't get there properly and if you release your normal-type ball, it will either miss the head pin or go on the nose or cross. So you give it a little extra lift and turn or hold back so it won't hook as much.

To me that's instinct, and every top bowler I have seen has it to some degree. Maybe it should be called a split-second adjustment instead of instinct. No matter. Much of this is done automatically, but it can be cultivated, too. Many times you can tell when things aren't just right, quickly think of the consequences and how to avoid them. There have always been arguments as to whether top athletes are born or made. I think there's something to both, so be aware of those last-second adjustments and call it instinct if you like. I do.

Reading Lanes

I like to keep things simple, and I've found that the more you know, the simpler things become. For instance, you must get a general idea of how lanes are acting or reacting before you can do your best on them.

ANGLES

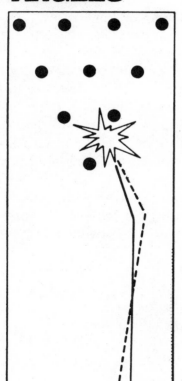

A bowler can roll from any angle on a lane, but there is always one that hits a certain lane better than another. Don't move from one angle to the other too quickly, but don't hesitate the minute you find that one angle carries the pins better than any other.

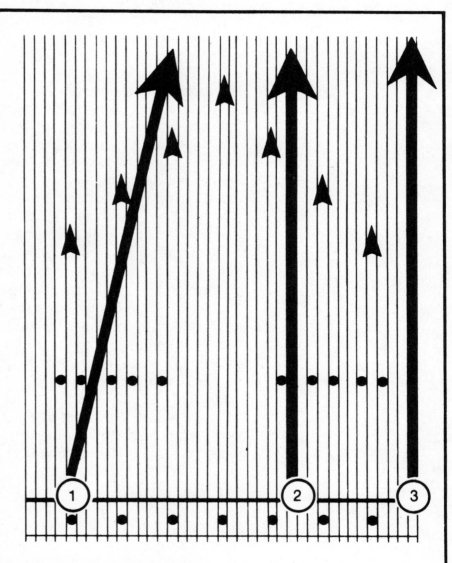

Angles—1) extreme inside, 2) normal, 3) extreme outside of gutter.

This takes a little homework, and sometimes detective work.

One of the best ways is to get to the lanes a little early and watch and listen. On the tour I will watch the most consistent bowlers, the ones who roll the ball almost the same each time and, of course, bowlers who roll a ball similar to the way I do. I don't hesitate to ask bowlers how the lanes are. You should do the same.

What I'm looking for is the breaking area of the lane, the part where I can get the best action for my ball. What do you do if you're in a strange place or there is no bowling or you don't know anybody or anything about the lanes?

First, try to find the track in the lane, the area used by most bowlers. In most cases the excessive wear on this section will make the track area darker. Also, because the dressing is removed, it will tend to have a dry, less-shiny look.

The track area can be as little as two boards or as much as six or even more. Normally it would be around the second arrow, possibly from the 9th to 15th boards. Once you find the track, it is best to play the left side of it, because if you make a slight error and miss your spot on the left, the ball will skid more and hold in the pocket; and if you miss your spot a bit on the right, you will be in the hooking area and the ball will have a good chance to get back.

We receive eight practice balls on the pro tour. In most amateur tournaments even less are allowed. So you must make them count. Watch your ball carefully from start to finish. Also watch the bowlers on the same lane, and you should get a general idea of the track area, and where it's best for you to bowl. Whenever in doubt, always go to what you feel is your best and most comfortable shot.

One of the problems faced by pros and all bowlers who must move to a new pair of lanes after each game is that each pair might be slightly different and slight adjustments might be needed. The same is true when you roll in an event in which you roll four or six games, then have the same amount of games off, then return for more bowling. Seldom are the lanes the same, so it becomes even more important to go through the same type of detective work.

Nothing hurts a bowler more than to have preconceived notions. In most cases, lanes will hook more as more games are rolled on them. But sometimes on the pro tour the patterns are such that as the tournament wears on they hook less. Always be prepared to make a move or make a change in your equipment. If you expect surprising situations, you will never be surprised.

Variables that affect a lane include humidity, inside and outside temperatures, amount of play, dressing penetration or movement, and the simple fact that each board of each lane is different.

A word here about bowling approaches. Approaches can be sticky or slippery, and either condition can give a bowler fits. Be prepared. If they are sticky, some steel wool will loosen them up. Ask to have it done. You should also have a stick applicator of a substance that will allow you to slide more easily. If you are sliding too much, there is probably an accumulation of dirt or dust. Make sure your shoes are always clean. Almost every pro is careful to wipe his shoes with a damp towel before bowling, and some do it on every shot. If you do find that the approaches are a bit tacky or slippery, you must accept it and do the best to alter your style a bit. Worrying and harping about a situation you can't change will only hurt you.

Adjusting

It would be wonderful if every lane worked the same way and all you had to do was to bowl the same way all the time. It would also be boring.

So adjustments must be made. A bowler, once he determines he has problems, should be prepared to make a move quickly. Don't do it after a single shot or two; it might be that you just aren't warmed up enough to roll the ball properly.

If you roll what you consider your normal ball and it doesn't quite reach the pocket, or it goes on the nose, a move is in order. If the ball is to the right of the target, then move to the right on the approach. Normally a board or two will do it for you, but you may have to move as many as five boards. This gives you a much better angle to the pins. You can also change the target. Stand in the same place with the same delivery but move your target a few boards to the left.

If your ball is going to the left then use the opposite procedure. Move your starting position to the left or the target to the right. Repeating, if the ball is going to the left of the pocket, move your starting point to the right or your spot on the lane to the left; and if the ball is going to the left, move your starting position to the left or your spot to the right.

The same result can often be obtained by slightly shifting the shoulders, causing you to face the target from a different angle. Again, if the ball is hooking too much, moving the shoulders right will help; if it's not hooking enough, shifting the shoulders left is helpful.

Speed of the ball can be used in adjustment, too. I'm fortunate in that I can roll the ball faster than 15 miles an hour and thus use that to cut a hook down. To me, Earl Anthony is the master of speed control. It has become natural to him because he spent countless hours, every day for years, perfecting this technique.

So, though speed is a way to adjust (more speed cuts a hook down, less allows for more hook), unless you have the delicate touch

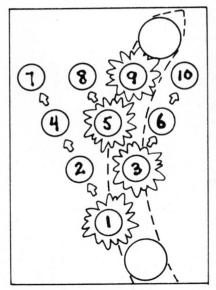

HERE IS A ROUTE
TRAVELED BY A PERFECT
RIGHT HANDED STRIKE BALL

100

required, it can be dangerous, because in trying to speed up or slow down you can alter other parts of your game.

The most popular way to adjust to hooking or nonhooking lane conditions among the pros is one of the easiest—just switching bowling balls. A softer-surface ball will grab more and give more hook, and a harder-covered ball will skid more and hook less.

Most pro bowlers and a great percentage of the higher-average amateur bowlers know how to bowl; and usually the difference is in what is known as *carrying the pins*. Three bowlers can roll a ball, all hit the pocket on hits that seem good. One will get a strike, another will leave a 10- or 4-pin, and another will leave a split.

Watch those pins, the way they do or don't go down. Like so many other things in bowling they, too, tell their own story. To me the key in carrying is the proper angle.

If you seem to be hitting the pocket and you're leaving the 5-pin or the 8 or 10 or 5–7 or 8–10, it's obvious that you need a ball coming in at more angle and should move so that the ball comes in more from the right.

On the other hand, if the line you are using produces the 4-pin or 4–7, known as a *fast eight,* or the frustrating 4–9 split, then your ball is driving into the pocket with too much angle and it should be cut by moving to the center or changing the spot.

Deflection is always present but never constant. Regardless of the weight of the ball or the angle, when the ball comes into contact with the wood, something has to give, and both do. The pins often fall grudgingly but not before they push the ball off to the right. How much depends on the weight of the ball and pins, the angle, and the lane conditions.

Lines, or angles, in bowling are vital. When you hear a pro say he's got the line, you can expect high scores. The gutter shot or what might be called the extreme outside line is rolled down the 1st or 2nd board; the outside line can range from the 1st to the 7th board; normal line from board 8 to about 15; tight line from 10 to 25; and deep inside from the 15th board to almost the opposite edge. Pros use all these lines from time to time, and some vary many boards from lane to lane on the same pair of lanes.

Remember, when adjusting, there are just four possible ways. The first is the best, by moving left or right on the approach and rolling the ball exactly the same way. The second is essentially the same, moving your target left or right. You can always attempt to hook the ball more or less, and finally you can speed up or slow down the ball. The latter two, though effective if executed well, are the most difficult, even for polished pros.

FRAME

7

STRIKES, SPARES, SPLITS AND MISSES

Despite what I and most of my fellow pros might feel, most perfect pocket hits result in strikes. We tend to think that somebody up there doesn't like us, that many of the hits we think should be strikes wind up with a pin standing somewhere. There are many millions who feel that whenever they pop the head-pin area pretty well, it should result in a strike. It just isn't that easy.

To achieve that perfect pocket hit, the ball must have the right amount of stuff or revolutions, the best possible angle and the proper speed. If you go by the book, the ball should be released over the foul line at about the second dot; it then rolls over the second arrow area; and once inside the 10 feet just before the pins, it begins and concludes its hook into the 1–3 pins, the pocket area, the 17th board.

The ball, on that perfect hit, knocks down only the 1-, 3-, 5-, and 9-pins. The six remaining pins are toppled by other pins, which is why angle and speed are so important. It is also the reason for many odd spare leaves. Pins don't always fall the way you might expect.

With perfect pinfall, the ball contacts the 1- and 3-pins, continues on to take out the 5- and 9-pins. The 1 hits the 2, which hits the 4, which takes out the 7. On the right side the 3 is banged into the 6, which pushes down the 10. The 8 falls when the 5 goes bouncing its way.

Many times the pins won't fall the way they were programmed. The 4 will often fly around or over the 7-pin, and the 6-pin often goes around the 10. You will see the number 8 pin on what seems like a perfect hit, and every now and then the 9 will stand. Sometimes it's because a pin is slightly off spot. Sometimes the weight of the pins or the lane condition can cause the problem. Many times it's the speed of the ball. However, pins fly and fall in different ways every time they're hit.

Accept the taps, the single pins that don't go down, in the same spirit you accept the lucky strikes that come your way. Or I should say, try to accept them. I've yet to meet a bowler who has felt he got as much as he hit for. In fact, most bowlers feel they can never get even with the pins, and that's one thing that keeps them coming back.

Hitting the pocket is the name of the game in bowling. Strive for accuracy, even at the expense of sacrificing part of a powerful working ball. If you are constantly around the pocket, you will score more than your share of strikes; and just as important, when you don't strike, the spares you leave will be the less-difficult ones.

There is no such thing as an easy spare. Though pros get plenty

103

of strikes, a little carelessness on a spare and they've tossed 11 or more pins away. I have watched top pros blow single pin spares because they take their minds off what they're doing and take the so-called easy spares for granted.

In my spare shooting I do two things I don't ordinarily do. I roll my ball straighter and with more speed. I don't believe in being cute or fancy on spares. You don't want to kill the pins or break them. In most cases you don't need any help from other pins; all you have to do is make sure that a piece of the bowling ball gets a piece of the pin.

Dr. George Allen is probably the world's greatest expert on spares. He has done extensive computer and mathematical analyses of all 1,023 possible spare leaves. He has combined all this with his own bowling experience and that of PBA Hall-of-Famer Dick Ritger to come up with the most scholarly explanation of spares ever.

Allen and Ritger have come up with ten items to consider in preparing for any spare leave. Before you ready yourself on the approach, you should determine the key pin and point of contact; select the target on the lane and the best angle; choose your approach position, taking into consideration lane condition, cross-lane angles, chop possibilities, and pin and ball deflection; and, finally, consider any special problems such as pins off spot, pin count, or the need to reduce or increase your angle.

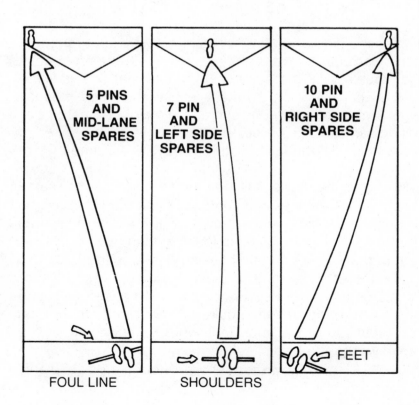

104

On the approach take your normal stance, face your target, recheck your approach position, take a deep breath, and count to three to avoid rushing. Concentrate on the shot, deliver the ball, watch it hit or miss your target, watch what happens to the ball and pins, and should you miss, decide what you did wrong and try to correct on the next spare.

There are a few key items in becoming a good spare bowler. First is to use the proper angle, and in spare shooting there are three general angles.

Any spares in the center of the lane, leaves in which the head pin or 5-pin are involved, are best shot by using your normal strike-ball angle. Spares on the 10-pin or right side are shot from the left, and spares on the 7-pin side or left are shot from the right. These angles give you the leeway to use as much of the lane as possible.

In every spare leave there is a key pin. When there is only one pin, it is the key pin. When there is more than one pin, you must determine the most important pin in the setup. Usually it's the pin nearest to you. But sometimes it's a pin that isn't even there. For instance, on the common baby split, the 3–10, the object is to hit the 3 and have it deflect into the 10. In essence you're actually trying to convert the missing 6-pin.

The same is true of the fit splits, the 4–5 or 5–6. When you go for them, the key pin in the 4–5 is the absent 2, while in the 5–6 it is the departed 3-pin.

In addition, always be wary of those pins in the dark, the sleepers, the hidden pins of double wood spares such as the 1–5, 2–8, and 3–9, and all combinations in which they pop up. Here is where pin and ball deflection enter the picture. When they meet, the ball bounces off and the pin gets knocked its merry way. Factors you must consider are weight of ball and pins, angle and speed of ball, the action imparted to the ball, and the existing lane conditions. That's why at times you must roll right at the pins and other times almost away from the pins to accomplish the same thing.

So every time you have a chance to hit every pin with the ball, that's the way to do it, particularly on such tricky spares as the 1–2–4, 1–2–4–7, 3–6, 6–10, and 3–6–10. Which brings up those real pests, the spares you are most likely to chop, knocking down the front pin of a spare leave and finding that a back pin or one to either side remains standing.

I have two spares I dread most, and I guess they rate as the two most pros would rather not leave. They are the bucket, the 2–4–5–8 (3–5–6–9 for lefties) and the 3–6–10. The problem is that if you use too much hook and the ball hooks sharply on many of these spares, such

LEFT SIDE SPARES

RIGHT SIDE SPARES

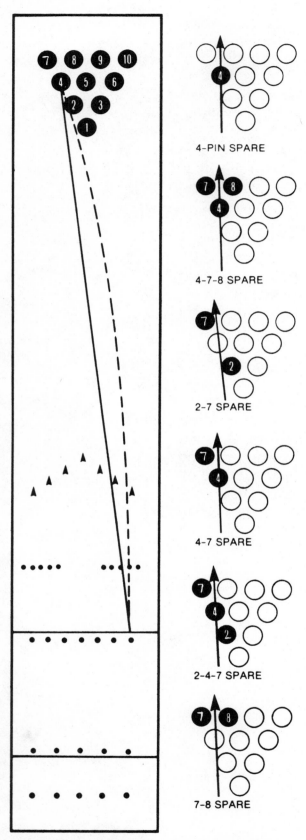

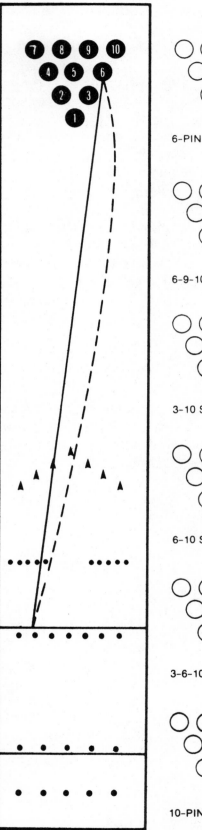

4-PIN SPARE

4-7-8 SPARE

2-7 SPARE

4-7 SPARE

2-4-7 SPARE

7-8 SPARE

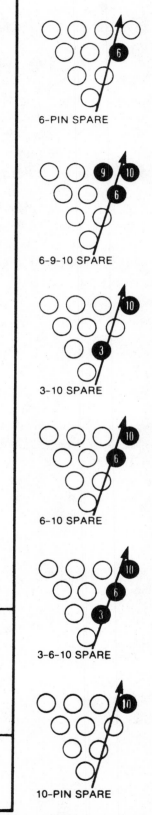

6-PIN SPARE

6-9-10 SPARE

3-10 SPARE

6-10 SPARE

3-6-10 SPARE

10-PIN SPARE

Solid line is straight ball, dotted line is hook ball.

Solid line indicates path of straight ball, dotted line indicates path of hook ball.

SPLITS

Converting the 4-5—Select a target to the right-center of the lane in order to connect squarely between the two pins. Accuracy is essential since the distance between pins is less than two inches narrower than the width of the ball.

The 5-7—Start from just right of center in order to hit the 5-pin on its right side causing it to deflect into the 7-pin.

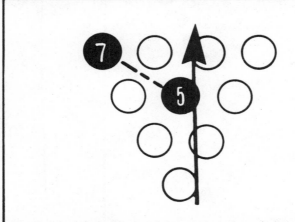

The 6-7—Very difficult, but possible to hook into the 6-pin on its right side (from the left side of the approach) causing it to skid across into the 7-pin.

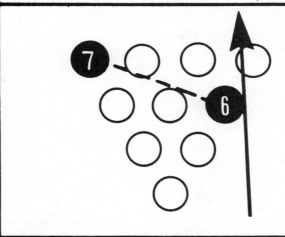

The 6-7-10—Same shot as the 6-7 with the ball taking out the 10-pin after deflecting the 6-pin into the 7-pin.

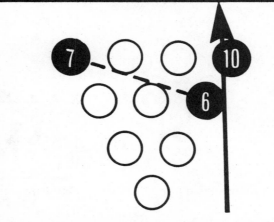

107

STRIKE BALL   # MIDDLE SPARES

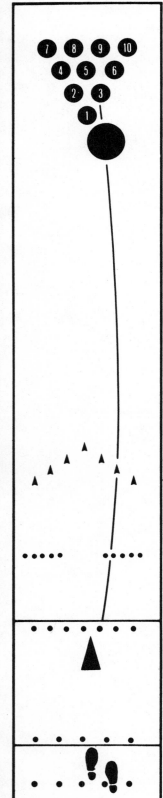

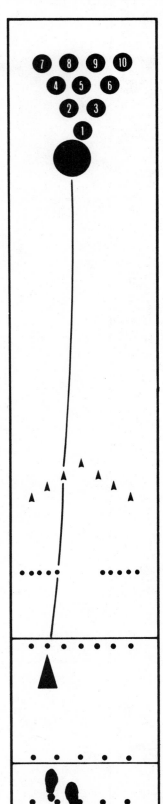

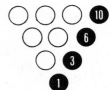

5-PIN SPARE

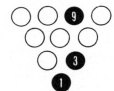

1-3-6-10 SPARE

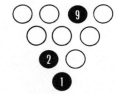

1-3-9 SPARE

1-2-9 SPARE

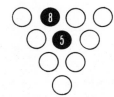

5-8 SPARE

1-2-5 SPARE

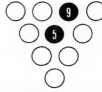

5-9 SPARE

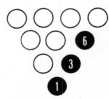

1-3-6 SPARE

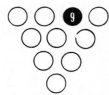

9 SPARE

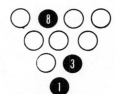

1-3-8 SPARE

Dart indicates finishing position of sliding foot   Dart indicates finishing position of sliding foot

as the 3–6–10, you take out the front pin, and if you ease up or take something off the ball, you slide by the front pin.

Your best bet is to roll the ball as straight as possible. Many spares, such as the 2–4–5, give you an option as to which side you shoot it from, left or right. Again, it's school time. Watch when other bowlers shoot the spare; pay attention when you must roll the ball in that area. The side that is easiest for you to roll from and the side from which you and your ball are most accurate is the side to use, and that could vary from lane to lane and in rare instances from game to game.

Speed certainly has an effect. In general, the faster you roll the ball, the straighter it will go. That makes extra speed good for single pins and double wood combinations. However, there is more chance to chop with more speed. The answer is to be consistent with your speed and learn what your ball does on certain spare leaves. Leave the speed switching to the pros or work into it gradually with plenty of practice.

Splits are spare leaves, too, but with a difference. There are gaps between the pins, and so you must either fit the ball between the pins or else slide one pin across a distance to topple the other. Often frustration is more of an enemy than the split, because many splits such as the 2–7, 3–10, 5–7, 5–10, 4–10, 4–7–10, 6–7, 6–7–10, and others can be converted, though with varying degrees of difficulty. Too many bowlers lose their tempers the minute they see a split and forget that they can be made. When they attempt to shoot the split, they practically forget everything but getting the ball down the lane quickly to forget the frame.

Though every split has been made at one time or another, the almost impossible splits—the 4–6, 7–9, 8–10, 7–10, and 4–6–7–10— are so rarely converted that in almost every case it makes more sense to be sure of the one or two pins you can make rather than to try to make the splits that are usually toppled only by flukes of pinfall.

And yet, after saying that, I must admit that I received more attention and publicity when I made the 7–10 split on national television than when I rolled a 299 game. I had calls from all over the country; experts were called to try to determine the odds on the 7–10 being made; and to this day when I get into any conversation, the 7–10 shot comes up. On its pretournament TV promos, the network shows my 7–10 being made. All I do on the almost-impossible ones is to roll the ball as hard and fast as I can, trying to hit it off the back cushion or the sideboards, just on the chance it might bounce right as that one shot did.

Whenever you're shooting a spare, keep the pin count in mind. For example, on many shots like the 5–7, sometimes missing both means you come closer to making the spare than to hit the 5-pin full. That's fine, but if you only need a pin to win the game, don't take any chances—hit that 5-pin full. Split making and whether to attempt to convert or not takes a little extra thought.

There are many methods to help you in shooting spares. One is the 3–6–9 system.

You have learned about your point of origin for a strike ball. The best place for you to start to hit the 1–3 pocket is usually slightly to the left of center on the approach. You will use your strike ball for center-lane spares. If you want to make the number 2 pin or left-side combinations with the 2-pin, simply move three boards to the right on the approach. That's three boards to the right, or where your foot started for a strike shot.

In making the 4-pin or combinations of the same, move six boards to the right of your strike origin. To convert the 7-pin, use the same idea by moving nine boards to the right.

Again, you use the same target you used for a strike but by changing where you start and then facing and swinging toward the spare target, you have changed the angle greatly without changing your normal style.

Using the 3–6–9 system for the right side is the same, with the exception that you must find your 10-pin conversion point of origin rather than the starting point for a strike. Take the third arrow area to the left of the 10-pin. Trace that back to the approach by creating an imaginary line to find the starting spot of your toe on the approach.

This gives you your point of origin for the 10-pin spare. For any 6-pin leaves or any combination of the 6-pin, just move three boards to the right on the approach. For number 3 pin spare combinations all you have to do is move six boards to the right of the original approach mark used to make the 10-pin.

I must caution you that though this system works well, you must always take into consideration such intangibles as lane conditions and your own style of bowling. There is no one best system; use this and others as guidelines to find what is best for you. You can use pin or spot

Opposite: *Position of ball as it enters into the 1-3 pocket for a strike.*

bowling for spares, but the same form of line bowling used on the strike ball works well, using an arrow and the point. This will also help you reach out, giving you a more consistent ball.

I have a tendency to get my ball well down the lane for spares, and I feel this helps me in making spares. Remember, the only easy spare is the one you don't have to shoot because you got a strike. Since no bowler scores strikes every time, study the spare leaves you run into most, figure out the best angles to convert them, and develop a spare shooting system best for you.

Spare shots can become a lesser challenge; and if you can make one extra spare a night, you can improve your average almost five points, and another spare each game and you could jump some 15 points.

On the next page are pictures showing the angle the ball should come into various typical spare leaves. The key is to always hit as many pins with the ball as possible. When it is not possible, then the best angle must be used to send pins flying into other pins. Half the battle of converting spares is knowing where to hit the pins.

FRAME

8

WINNING THINKING

There's one area of the game I had little trouble developing, and that's winning thinking. I have always liked winning. I have always felt that if you're not out to win, then you should stay home.

Knowledge is one thing. Physical ability is another, and included in that is the ability to concentrate, but if you don't develop a winning attitude, you're just not going to win.

On our pro tour there are more than 100 of the world's best bowlers who roll regularly, more than 15 weeks of the more than 30-week schedule. I would say that all of them are capable of winning if you judged them on native ability and knowledge.

But there is a wide gap in their thinking. In every tournament during the match play you will run into a game where you get a bad break or two and your opponent gets a good break, and he beats you even though you out-bowled him. I have had various bowlers tell me they are sorry they beat me. To me they are losers. Don't be sorry when you win, no matter how you win. Certainly, be realistic; if you have a lucky win, admit it if you must, but never feel sorry.

I make no bones about it; when I'm in competition, I'm at war. I'm out to kill and burn those pins. My opponent is my enemy. I don't talk to him unless I must. I'm not rude in any way, but I'm all business because bowling is my business. I block out as much as I can except the game.

Many feel that I get up too quickly. They're wrong. Though I only take up to four seconds to get off and bowling, I have carefully planned and thought out my shot. Once I get on the approach my only thought is to hit my target; so once I zero in with my eyes, have my feet placed the way I want and my fingers in the ball feeling good, it's time to go. I think bowlers foul themselves up when they take too much time. I say take all the time you need but not a second more.

There's nervous tension in every bowler going for a key shot, whether it's in a shop or church league or on national TV for many thousands of dollars. The best way to fight that pressure is to concentrate on your target.

Concentration is the most needed asset in executing the basic fundamentals of bowling, regardless of the individual styles used. Many bowlers seem to be too busy or too lazy to work on concentration and winning thinking. For many it's the fatal error that prevents winning.

Mental imaging is a favorite device used by pros. Even the world's worst bowler has at one time or another rolled a perfect strike, made most of the difficult spares, and even converted an almost impossible split. When you need one of those perfect rolls, think about how many times you have done it and tell yourself you need only do it one more time.

In those seconds before rolling the ball, think deeply about the shot coming up, picturing the mental image of yourself and the ball and how you accomplished the perfect shot so many times before, or even once before. Some bowlers are almost in a trance and probably wouldn't recognize their own mothers during those few seconds before a shot. I doubt if I would.

In the clutch many bowlers pull the shot. Call it a choke shot if you wish, but there's a simple way to turn this minus into a plus. Play a light pocket on a key shot. Then, if you release the ball normally, you will have a chance to carry a light hit strike; and if you pull it, the ball will go solidly in the pocket.

There's still a bowling term used called *playing safe.* It refers to a situation when a bowler needs a mark, a strike, or spare in the final frame to win. The playing-safe school of thought is to miss the head pin, thus leaving a so-called safe to convert a spare. There is no such animal. When you need a mark, go for a strike. When you try to leave an easy spare, you usually leave anything but.

There isn't too much in the way of strategy bowling, but there are such things as choice of lanes, line-up placement in doubles or team play, or maybe little attempts at bench jockeying or psyching out an opponent.

If you have a choice of lanes, and on TV one bowler or the other always has such a choice, the decision is two-fold. First, do you want to finish first; and second, is there a particular lane on which you want to finish.

If you feel you want the final frame pressure to be on your opponent, so be it. If you like the idea of being able to decide your own fate on the lane rather than the bench, then you take the final slot. However, in most cases, if you have a choice of lanes, your best bet is to select the lane you hit best to finish on, regardless of whether that choice forces you to finish first or last.

Bowlers don't have many weapons with which to throw off another bowler. The main attempts are to hurt your pace. If you like to bowl fast, they try to slow down the pace. Some can talk to you or others to get your mind away from the game. In the pro ranks you are allowed to rerack the pins if you feel they're off spot. Some players use the limit in match play whether they need them or not. I have known bowlers to drop items on purpose, sit or stand in such a position as to cast a shadow that might disturb an opponent, or even use the evil eye stares that boxers seem to think work.

I can offer only this word of advice: either ignore it all or attempt to use the same tactics. I feel ignoring is the best method unless an opponent does something illegal; then you blow the whistle. If your opponent finds his antics don't bother you, they usually end up bothering him.

Always bowl in as many different situations as you can. Always bowl to win. This will give you experience in winning. When you win or roll well enough to win, you gain confidence. Once you learn the proper concentration that is fortified by good past performances and experience, you have the winning thinking.

But there are times when you can out-think yourself. My good friend Johnny Petraglia was rolling an exhibition match in a small town, bowling against one of the local stars. Usually Petraglia would give the local bowler a handicap to make things even. That night the opponent said he wanted no handicap except three "gotchas." Not knowing what a "gotcha" was, but not wanting to appear stupid, Petraglia agreed.

The first game began and Petraglia took a good lead by starting with five strikes in a row. As Petraglia leaned in to go for his sixth strike, his opponent rushed up behind him, slapped him on the rear, and yelled, "Gotcha."

From then on a shaken Petraglia rolled badly and lost. "I could never get set for the rest of the night," he moaned later. "I was always waiting for the next 'gotcha.'"

Use Bowling

Use bowling, don't let it use you. Bowling is a fun game, and to this day I love it. But don't let it dominate you. Use it as an outlet to rid yourself of some of your aggression. Make believe those pins are what's bothering you, and you'll be surprised how much better you feel when you knock some down.

Want to meet people? There's no better place than bowling. You can meet and get to know people of all ages, every ethnic group, every educational and financial class. Join a group or a league at your nearest or favorite bowling center. They will do their best to place you at the time of the day or night you wish to bowl.

If you want to use bowling as a quickie exercise, you can always get a game or two during your lunch hour or right after work or any time of the day or night. It's been said that during every minute of every day, someone somewhere in the world is bowling.

If you want to make bowling a career, you can have your cake and eat it too by testing the waters on a part-time basis, first by combining work or profession with bowling on weekends.

Decide how much you want to give to bowling and how much you want to take, and, surprisingly, you can work it out. Bowling is many different things to many different people.

One psychologist offered this advice to a nervous patient, "If you bowl a lot, cut it down a little. If you don't bowl, take it up."

Slumps

Because the bowling season never ends, every bowler runs into bad stretches much the way a baseball player can fall into a slump. It's easy to panic. If you're a league bowler, your teammates hope you get sick. If you're a pro you might not eat very well until the slump ends.

What do you do?

First, check your equipment to see that it's okay. Then check yourself to discover if you are having any special medical problems or if there are some personal worries. Next, go over your game carefully to pinpoint the problem. Is your ball going too much left or right, hooking too much or not enough? Are you missing more spares than usual? Which ones?

After acting like a detective, and usually another bowler can help, do one of two things. Either go to a center where you know you can bowl well, and bowl as much as you can on lanes you like until you score well and rebuild your confidence. Or just take a rest—lay off.

If all else fails, don't push that panic button. Since bowling keeps you active for such a long stretch, ride it out. Even if you can't find a reason for the slump, have patience, and in most cases it will leave as mysteriously as it came.

Ed. note. Mark Roth is one of the most slump-free bowlers in the history of bowling. He once cashed in 86 of 87 tournaments (that's a span of three years), and he can't remember when he failed to cash in two tournaments in a row.

Johnny Petraglia, a neighbor of Mark Roth's in New Jersey, won his first title as a teenager, served in Viet Nam, then came back to establish himself as one of the top names in the sport.

JOHNNY PETRAGLIA

FRAME

9

ALL FOR BOWLING
AND BOWLING FOR ALL—
SPECIAL TIPS FOR
SPECIAL PEOPLE

The Child Bowler

There is no age limit to bowling, but there should be some guidelines. Just as soon as a boy or girl can handle a light bowling ball, and some are as light as 8 pounds, they should be allowed to bowl.

First, give them a little instruction as to the operation of the equipment; show them how to put fingers in the ball, point out the arrows, and let them bowl. Be there to supervise, but don't attempt to really teach a three- or four-year-old. As they roll more, they will ask you for help. Then bring them along slowly and with patience.

As soon as they are ready, enter them in junior bowling leagues. Again, don't push them. It's my feeling that in most cases you can't get into deep instruction until the youngster is ten or eleven. Let the young bowler go his own pace. In the beginning, let them have fun without worrying about more than the bare basics.

A bowler is never too young to have his own personal equipment. Here, special care must be taken since the young bowlers grow out of shoes and bowling balls almost yearly. Once into the juniors, guide the young bowlers to proper instruction sources; watch them bowl without being a coach or a critic; encourage them to roll in tournaments; and if you have the time, bowl with them in an adult–child league. Always remember, adult bowlers serve as models for the youngsters. Many times when they do something wrong it's only because they are copying something an older bowler shouldn't have done.

Older Bowlers

There are many bowlers from age sixty to ninety who are just as active, just as interested, and just as keenly competitive as the pros. But sometimes they expect too much and sometimes must make some concessions.

As you get older, don't hesitate to go to a lighter ball. Take shorter steps, cut down the approach, and slow up the pace. If it's easier to spot closer to the foul line, do it.

If there are physical problems with fingers, arms, legs, or feet, it is easy enough to work around them. Different grips can ease pressure in different areas in the use of the bowling ball, and minor adjustments in style can overcome most problems. There is no reason why any bowler of any age can't enjoy bowling. I've found that most of the seniors I know try harder than the average bowler. And many can still roll the way they always have.

In that case, don't make any changes until they become necessary.

Bowling is a game for all, but few have mastered it so well as PBA Hall of Famer Buzz Fazio, who could still roll with and against the best at age 70. His motto always was to use what talent you have in the best way possible.

Tall Bowlers, Short Bowlers

In talking to some of the great tall bowlers of our time, including Dave Soutar, Dave Davis, Gary Dickinson, Frank Ellenburg, and Steve Cook, the consensus is that big men must be careful not to bring their bodies up too quickly during the approach and must concentrate on keeping the finishing knee properly bent.

Ellenburg notes that if you keep your feet close to the floor as you take your steps, you will be less likely to jump up. Pretending that there is something sticky on your feet that will act like glue should help keep your feet and body down.

Most tall bowlers lean forward at the start. In order to offset this problem a good practice is to lean back a little more than normal at the beginning, which is what Dave Davis does. Some feel that too wide a span in your bowling ball gives you too much feel and allows a big man to roll the ball too fast too easily.

At six feet, six inches and more than 260 pounds, Cook is the biggest pro on tour; and he sums it up best when he emphasizes, "Since you can't do too much about the way you are built, then you work with it."

Bowlers on the short side have more difficulty generating power and their reach is limited, but they are closer to the floor and don't have to worry too much about getting low and into the shot at the finish.

Thin bowlers have an advantage in that they have no hips to speak of and can keep the ball-and-arm-swing closer to the body. Strong bowlers can utilize speed, while those not-so-strong bowlers can easily develop a better working ball.

What it all boils down to is that there is a best and basic way to do everything, and then there is a best way to do everything within your own physical structure. Make the two meet. It can be done. Among the honored members of the American Bowling Congress Hall of Fame are Allie Brandt, barely five feet tall and 100 pounds, and Billy Welu, who soared at six feet, five inches and weighed more than 240 pounds.

Women Bowlers

I don't know why, but I'm often asked if a good female pro is able to compete with a top male pro. At this time the answer is no, because as in other areas women haven't had equal opportunity.

The women pros haven't had the same chance as the men to learn through experience, because their tour has been short and sporadic. They don't get used to rolling 40 to 60 games a week in competition. Very few of them can make a living just through bowling, so, as a result, their livelihood doesn't depend on bowling. Therefore, in my opinion, very few have developed any kind of killer instinct; and to me they seem too polite to each other in competition. Maybe if their tour was solid and offered more money, things would change.

Don't get me wrong; there are many fine women bowlers, and for a game or two they can beat any male pro. But over the long run they wouldn't make it, because they haven't been tested in long, grinding tournaments. They are still in the learning process of pro bowling that men went through more than ten years ago.

The average woman bowler should be more serious about the game. I urge them to learn more about the sport, about equipment, about techniques. On the league and amateur level there is no reason why women can't compete almost equally with men. In many cases they do.

Women can use the same techniques as men, but women will have a tendency to roll a backup ball because the female arm is constructed differently from a male's, and it gives them a swing that is more natural for a backup ball. Since the backup is the least desired type of ball, a woman must work a bit harder to perfect a hook ball.

Women are in general shorter and lighter than men, so they should lean to shorter steps and shorter approaches. They should be very careful about the weight of the bowling ball but not go too heavy or too light. Though the full 16-pound limit isn't vital, most women can handle a 16- or at least a 15-pound ball. There is no reason to go to an extremely light ball such as 10 pounds.

More than half the bowlers in the country are now women, and the most popular bowling leagues are mixed leagues featuring teams of men and women.

Many of the nation's top coaches, in junior leagues, in high schools, and in colleges, are women. They play a vital role in all of bowling, and their only weak point seems to be in the development of the pro side of the sport.

Left-handers

Almost since the time I went out on tour there has been much talk and argument about whether or not left-handers have an advantage. In some cases they do, but in some cases the right-hander has an advantage, too. It's all in the nature of the sport.

For many years left-handed bowlers had great problems. The right side of a lane always developed a track giving the right-handers a good area to get action on the ball. The left side, used a lot less, had no track; so, in effect, the southpaws were rolling on a brand new lane all the time, which is usually much tougher to score on. But what used to be a disadvantage for the lefties became an advantage. In many cases

124

the track on the right side was virtually unplayable, while the left side was true and consistent. In any given situation one side or the other might be better.

For basic instructional techniques a lefty can use the same instruction given right-handers and reverse it. In general, the lefties must move more to the outside in order to gain more angle to overcome the portion of the lane that usually hooks less. Because they have had to make their own tracks on most occasions, most southpaws will develop a ball with more lift and turn. They will do what they must to keep the ball in action. Some even rough up the track of the bowling ball so it will grip better.

If you are a lefty be aware that your side of the lane is different and that it may help or hurt. Don't be overly impressed by an easy lane or completely dismayed when they seem so tough compared to the righties.

I consider Bill Allen, Dave Davis, Mike McGrath, Marty Piraino, Earl Anthony, Johnny Petraglia, and Mike Aulby to be great bowlers, not just great left-handed bowlers. I seem to roll well when the lefties do and often find myself in the finals with half a dozen of them or more, and they sure are tough.

I would love to see the day when some type of lane surface is perfected so that there is no difference in condition, which would mean the end of the lefty-righty confrontation.

Handicapped Bowlers

If you are handicapped in any way, it shouldn't stop you from bowling. In the bowling family there are such organizations as the American Blind Bowling Association, American Wheelchair Bowling Association, and the National Deaf Bowling Association.

The American Bowling Congress and Women's International Bowling Congress allow special equipment to be used by the handicapped, and pro shop owners and managers consider it a worthy challenge to come up with the proper answer to any equipment problem. A handicapped person should check with the local bowling center or local bowling association for full information on the services available to them.

"Bowling is truly a sport for all people," says Bill Bunetta, a great bowler who went on to become a noted teacher. Bunetta, in his constant travels for AMF, has found the one-step delivery to be a boon to many who suffer from various leg problems.

"The bowler's stance should be comfortable and relaxed, feet parallel, about an inch and a half apart. The foot opposite the bowling arm should be about five inches behind the other. The ball is held

*Blind bowlers are using guide rails in the photo but some simply use
the buddy system in which a sighted bowler sets them up properly for
each shot. There are various ways in which handicapped persons can learn
and continue to bowl. Bowling organizations are constantly searching for
new and better methods and mechanical devices to aid the handicapped.*

directly below the shoulder with shoulders over the knees and head up. Push the arms straight forward, keeping the arm relaxed and the wrist fairly straight.

"Swing the arm to roughly eye level, then back in a natural arc to about shoulder height, then forward again to eye level. When the arm comes forward, also slide ahead on the foot opposite the bowling arm. Both arm and foot should move at the same time with shoulders level and body facing straight ahead."

Moderate practice with and without a bowling ball, and adjustments made to fit each individual case will result in any bowler being able to accomplish the one-step delivery in a short period of time.

For those confined to wheelchairs, Lindy Faragalli, who bowled against those so confined under the same condition, advises: "You find that some of the basic fundamentals can't be used, so in some cases the often-frowned-upon out-and-in swing becomes a necessity. Finding a way to swing the ball is important. A ball fit that is secure, yet easy to release, is helpful."

Blind bowlers can use special guide rails, with the aid of a sighted bowling buddy, to position them and call out spare leaves. Some blind bowlers manage with just a friend when the rails are not available. Blind bowlers often know what pins are liable to be left standing by the sound the ball makes on contact with the pins.

Frank Gallo, the first deaf pro bowler, explains, through signs and notes, that it can be an advantage to be deaf. "You are able to concentrate more on what you are doing because you aren't distracted; and because you use your hands so much, you develop a finer sense of feel than the average person, and feel is important in bowling. However, you must make sure that you visually observe what is going on about you so that you obey the rules of bowling courtesy. Don't become so absorbed that you balk other bowlers."

Teaching Handicapped Bowlers

The first step in helping handicapped bowlers is to honestly accept limitations. Equipment must be chosen with care, with the accent on lighter balls, simple grips, and sturdy, comfortable shoes.

In dealing with individuals who have problems with coordination, keep it as simple as possible. Make sure the proper fingers are in the proper holes. Keep checking, particularly with those who are slower mentally and have trouble keeping their minds on one thing for a long period of time. I have found that all are apt students, mainly because everything comes tough to them; so they are more than willing to try harder, over and over again.

Nothing beats patience in bowling, and patience is a virtue most handicapped persons have in abundance. I have worked with many groups and many ages. If they can't see the pins they develop a way to hear them go down. If they can't hear they see more details than most. If they can't run or walk they settle for crawling or just standing or lying at the foul line.

Teaching or helping handicapped bowlers calls for common sense. Try to stick to the basics in as simple a form as possible, but be elastic, sacrifice power for comfort, never insist on doing things one way, inspire and encourage, not embarrass. Never use any mechanical device that in any way could injure the bowler or do damage to the lane equipment.

The rewards can't be calculated. When that bowler knocks pins down, no matter how few, and gives you a great big smile, no bank vault is big enough to hold such worth.

Dave Davis, long one of the premier lefties in the sport and a New Jersey neighbor of Mark Roth, is a PBA Hall of Famer and a top instructor as well as a bowler. Known as one of the deep concentrators in the sport, he advises all bowlers to pay close attention to what they do and what they fail to do when they bowl. Davis feels that bowlers should concentrate on their own game, not worry about opponents. Your good scores will cure all.
Opposite: Jim Worth is a good bowler despite the loss of a leg and he now teaches other bowlers how to overcome their handicaps. He travels across the country for the National Bowling Council.

128

FRAME

10

MOST COMMON MISTAKES

The perfect picture bowler has yet to be born and those looking for such will find just that, a good picture, but maybe not the best bowler.

I have seen many pros, well aware they do things the so-called wrong way, work hard to correct them, finally do things the way they're supposed to be done, and see their scores go down. When Wayne Zahn changed his high back swing to a more normal one, he had a bad year; and when he returned to his natural way, he got back on the ball.

I know I drift in my approach, something you definitely should not do; but I also adjust to take into consideration that I do drift and compensate by using a different target. I also take six steps, even though I recommend four. Actually, my first two steps are almost like getting myself into motion for the four-step delivery.

What I am saying is, be yourself. Don't try to go strictly by the book unless that is your natural way. Most of the time, by the time a bowler looks for help from a professional instructor or from some of the good printed material, he has already formed many habits. Some can be changed. In fact, if you have any major trouble you should change. But you can't change you. Your physical make-up, your mental attitude, your ability to adjust must all be taken into consideration.

Teata Semiz used to roll an extremely big hook. He decided he should cut it down. It took him more than a year. How many bowlers have the time or inclination to go through such a change-over?

What happens is that bowlers make do, and sometimes one error is corrected by another error. However, that still doesn't change the fact that a simple look at your game can go a long way.

In your starting position, don't hold the ball too high or too low, and don't stand too close or too far from the foul line. Relax, keep your feet flat and toward the target, and the same for your shoulders. Get your hand well into the ball with the weight resting on the nonbowling hand, and make sure the ball is to the right of the center of your body. Knees should be slightly bent; and once you feel you're ready, get going in a few seconds.

On your steps keep the first one short and then let them get longer as you go on. Your contact should be heel first and then toe except for your final slide, when the toe hits first. Don't hop, jump, or leap; your feet should hardly leave the floor. It's a walk to the line, not a running race.

The best arm swing is a straight one, so keep your elbow close to the hip, don't drop your shoulders, keep a good grip on the ball, but don't clutch it, and don't try to force the ball with power.

As you move through the approach, keep your shoulders in the line of the shot. Get lower as you get to the line, with no jerky bends of the knee or waist but with the body solid and in control. Keep your head level, eyes on target. When you are in the last step, make sure you're well planted before you let the ball go; and if you can let the ball go at a point lower than the knee and reach out toward the target, you will be comfortable and on your aim.

Just paying attention to those simple items will do much to help you avoid the common mistake of rushing the line, lofting the ball, dropping the ball, pulling the ball, in and out swings, poor follow through, and pushaway problems such as moving the ball too fast or slow.

When you discover errors in your game, you will find them at the line; but to correct them you will have to trace back to their point of origin.

This brings us to the common error of too many coaches. You should find a good coach, preferably a pro; but a friend, teammate, or even a relative that knows your game well will be of great benefit. They can easily see if your approach position, ball position, steps, or arm swing have changed appreciably from when you roll well. The keys to good bowling are simple; to have ball and foot arrive at the foul line at the same time, the ball being brought there by a straight arm swing which allows the bowler to release the ball consistently.

You would be surprised how one correction can often eliminate a number of errors. For instance, an improperly fitted bowling ball can cause you to loft the ball, drop the ball, bend your elbow, roll the ball too fast or too slow, and rip your fingers or thumb.

Pro instructors estimate that 75 percent of the success of your game is tied up in your timing—the way you manage to coordinate your arm and foot movements—15 percent in your form and release at the line, and 10 percent in the type of ball you roll.

All that points up is that you must get there properly, otherwise you are almost gone. Once you get to the line correctly, it's much easier to release the ball well; and if you do that, no matter what kind of ball you roll, if it's on target it will score.

I have another little switch from the norm that people often notice: I tuck my pinky on the ball. I do it for good reason—it gives me more lift on the ball. I started doing it when I was very young and it stuck, so I continued. I'm not the only one who does this, but the majority spread their pinky and index finger. Some keep the noninserted fingers close to the holes, while others spread them as far as they can, using them almost as adjustable rudders to give a little more or a little less lift to the ball.

The 10-pin is a tough spare, and many bowlers balk when the ball return is to their left. Here Mark Roth shows the best angle to use to solve both.

133

FRAME

11

BACK TO THE BASICS
AND PRACTICE, PRACTICE, PRACTICE

One important aspect we haven't discussed so far is practice. People often ask when I practice, how much I practice, and exactly how I practice.

Most of them are surprised when I tell them that when I'm on tour, I do very little practicing. The reason for that is I'm too busy bowling. If you make the finals of a tournament, you are bowling five straight days. If you don't make the finals, you roll three days.

Prior to the tour I will probably roll a few hours every day to get into the shape I want to get into; then I just need a minimal amount of games. Other pros roll as many as 40 or 50 games a day. The main fact to remember is that every one of the pro bowlers, in order to get where they are, had to roll many thousands of games. I doubt if any of them rolled less than 100 games a week for years.

Where does that put the average bowler? It puts him in a position of being forced to make his practice sessions count. I used to practice in a bowling center that had four sides. I would personally do the lanes, all with a different lane condition; and I would practice a few games on each, then move from one lane condition to another.

You can do the same thing on a more modest scale. Pick and choose where you practice. Go to a different center each time to get yourself familiar with different conditions. Practice only as long as you can concentrate, be it minutes or hours.

I prefer practicing on tougher lane conditions where I really have to work to roll 200 to 215. I feel that if you can master the tougher scoring centers then you'll go big in an easier scoring house. Some bowlers prefer to roll on easy lanes, feeling they can get grooved in; and once they have the physical movements down they can conquer any condition.

I also practice spare shooting. If you can arrange with a center to have a pin chaser help you and set up your most difficult spares, fine. If not, just practice your various spare angles at the full setup of pins.

In general, don't keep score because it might distract you from your primary purpose, that of attempting to solve a single problem. Don't try to correct or work on more than one thing at a time unless they naturally go together. Practice alone or with someone to help you—someone who will help, not socialize.

Never practice so many games that you become tired or wind up with aching, cut, or bruised fingers or thumb; but if you must bowl in a long tournament, bowl the games you will have to bowl just to learn how to pace yourself.

If you get a new ball, try it out before you use it in competition. Odds are it will be just fine, but it may need some minor sanding or alteration.

Don't be afraid to make changes in your game, but do so only to help, only because you have the yen to or have been advised to make a change, and only if you are willing to work hard. One of the great boons to practice is the use of video-tape machines, and more and more centers feature them.

Harry "Tiger" Smith, a PBA Hall-of-Famer, rolled every ball in practice as though it meant a national championship because he felt some day it might. He recalls, "It got so that the more I practiced the better I got; but the better I got, the more I had to practice."

Courtesy

The rules of courtesy and good manners are important in bowling, despite the fact they're not bound into a rigid code.

First, respect the equipment—yours, that of the other bowlers, and the expensive equipment the center must maintain for you to bowl. Never use anyone's personal ball or even stick your fingers into it without asking permission first. We all have our own brand of dust and perspiration, and it could be just enough to foul up the other ball.

Don't bring food and drink to the scoring table. If it spilled in the wrong place, it could be dangerous. Don't stamp cigarettes out on the rug, place gum beneath the chairs, or litter in any way.

When two bowlers are ready to roll at the same time, the bowler on the right has the green light. It should not be a race. Don't stand on the approach unless you are going there to bowl; and if you must wait, signal nearby bowlers to go ahead of you. Once you bowl, stay in the confines of your lane. First, because that's the way it's supposed to be; and second, you could get hurt or hurt someone else if your body-english gyrations steer you in the path of another bowler armed with a bowling ball.

A bowler should always be on time for a league or tournament bowling, otherwise he causes trouble for other people and gets a zero or a lower score than his average for the missed frames. In the same vein, a bowler should always be ready to bowl when it is his turn. If you want to talk, wander, drink, or watch television, do it on your own time without wasting the time of others.

Though there is always a place for a zinger or two, deep needling, loud heckling, griping and profane language, or obscene gestures are out of place, and so are the ones who use them. Don't be critical; give help only when asked but feel free to ask for help from others.

Don't try to show how macho you are by trying to impress by throwing the ball as fast and as high as you can. You will probably dent the lane, throw your arm out, and lose friends as well as scores. Even if you do get some bad breaks, don't take your bad score out on your teammates or by bouncing the ball or kicking or punching. You will hurt your hand or foot and sportsman reputation.

Do your best to win, want to win, but realize that for every winner there are many losers. Accept winning or losing as best you can. It won't be too important 100 years from now.

Equipment

Always keep checking and rechecking your bowling ball, bag, and shoes. The ball is the most important, and this you should leave to an expert. Don't feel too secure once you have a ball. You change, you gain or lose weight, and that changes your size. Learn how to use tape or inserts so that you can change the size of the holes. The tape should be applied in short strips just below the lip of the holes in the exact area you want filled. It should be removed the same way. Short strips give great flexibility.

Don't leave your bowling ball in a sweltering or freezing car trunk. If it's a soft surface ball, it will become illegally soft or it will practically freeze and begin to sweat when you get it to the lanes.

Shoes and bags wear out. Don't get the last possible bit of wear from them. Every day more and more bowling aids are on the market. Some are put there after years of research and development, while others seem like they might have been dreamed up on the way home after a New Year's Eve party. Pick and choose carefully.

Every bowler is seeking a magic grip. There is no such dream come true. What you must seek in a grip is a comfortable hold on the ball, one that will allow you to carry the ball easily and allow you to swing and release the ball efficiently with the least amount of waste motion. That applies no matter what the grip. I would strongly advise either the conventional or full-fingertip. In the conventional you put your fingers all the way in the holes to the second joint, while with the fingertip it's to the first joint.

I do not advise the so-called semi-fingertip, because there the finger goes in to a point between the joints and this could lead to inconsistency.

Steps

As mentioned previously, the largest percentage of the attributes necessary for good bowling are tied up in how you get to the line. You must determine where you will start, how many steps you will take, the size,

In the photo sequences on the next three pages Mark Roth shows
his versatility by making his shots and then moving out of the
way quickly so that the viewer can see the line of the ball as
it makes its way down the lane toward the pocket.

In this final picture of the group, Roth is completely to the left as the ball is about to enter the 1-3 pocket. If this were in competition he would be rooting it home in some form of body English. As Mark is doing, always watch the ball all the way.

timing, direction, and height from the floor. Once you're set and you know the number of steps, it becomes your task to put the ball and foot into motion, then bring the arm down with little help from you, utilizing the shoulder as your aiming guide.

They can say all they want about a devastating ball, but accuracy is still the key in bowling. And the key to accuracy is to do the same thing over and over again until the approach becomes almost second nature. The less thinking you must do, the better.

The release is of great importance because it happens quickly and leads to the explosion point. The swing ends at the latter part of the down swing, and that's when the release comes into being.

To me the follow-through is a continuation of the swing—it helps you go through the ball, aids in the accuracy needed to hit your target, and prevents several problems. We talked about line bowling, where you set two targets on the lane and go over both. You can draw those same types of imaginary lines in the air so that once you release the ball, you can then reach for the other target in the air and guarantee yourself a steady follow-through. I think the most interesting challenge of bowling comes in figuring out the best methods of targeting, reading lanes, and making adjustments.

In earlier chapters it was explained how you can go about the various methods, and then it becomes a judgment call. Oddly, one of the appeals of pro bowling is the fact that you are all alone on that lane. You must make your own decision.

If you roll the ball badly, no outfielder in the world can save you with a good catch. If you throw a foul, you don't get a second chance. There are few judgment calls by officials that can alter your performance. You are master of your fate. For me, and for most people, that's good. There's a great feeling of accomplishment when you do it by yourself, even if you have had help from others in learning; in how to best execute, you still must do it yourself.

Pro bowlers do not earn salaries. What they earn is what they win. If they work badly one week, and that means bowling badly, they don't get paid. So it is with all bowlers. The reward is there, but only if you work.

A new bowler may be happy to get a strike and a spare and shoot a 100 game. But soon he or she wants two strikes and two spares for a 120. The pros average six or more strikes to get their 200-plus averages, and they won't be satisfied until they shoot 300 every game.

Bowling is a sport that seems amazingly simple, and is, on the surface. But the more you bowl, the more it challenges both your body and mind. Some great athletes have tried bowling and enjoyed it tre-

One of the things a pro bowler must learn is that there is more to bowling than just bowling, and TV interviews before and after matches are important. It can be pleasant, as Roth discovered after winning so many titles on TV. It makes the job easier to take.

143

mendously, until they got serious and found out how tough it is on the pro level. But that's what bowling is all about. You can be your own key to how far you want to go by devoting the necessary time, effort, and even expense to climb the bowling ladder. You can practice on the lanes or even at home, using whatever is available. I used to set up a pillow and roll my bowling ball against it. To practice your swing and approach, you can use an iron, or a beer or soda can.

And, of course, you must have a sense of humor. Bowling can be a funny game, even if it wasn't meant to be. I always liked the attitude of Norm Meyers, a fine pro who, though he cashed regularly and won a title, never made it big.

One of the crosses Norm had to bear is the fact that he is Dick Weber's brother-in-law and too many times the references to Meyers mentioned that fact rather than his obvious ability. Weber, the all-time great from St. Louis, seemed to be particularly tough whenever he met his brother-in-law, rolling a number of 300s against him.

After a particularly tough loss to Weber in the final game of a pro tournament, a well-wisher told Norm, ''Don't take it too hard, it was God's will.''

And Meyers replied, ''I know, I just rolled against him.''

Caring for your equipment is easy and it helps. Such simple things as cleaning your ball when needed are shown by Roth as he prepares. A ball can easily pick up surface dust, and it can be just as easily wiped off with your towel or with ball cleaner.

FRAME
12

MARK ROTH
ANSWERS QUESTIONS

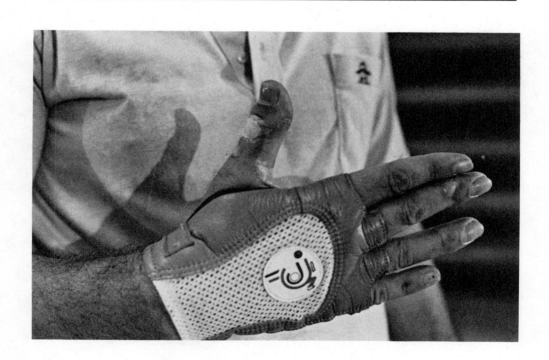

Q. What is Marshall Holman really like, and how did you pair up as doubles partners?

A. People see Marshall as a guy who snarls at the pins, punches at the air, and makes gestures that aren't always fit for Sunday school. I see him differently—as a friend, a dedicated, intelligent, and sometimes funny guy. It's just that he goes all out in the only way he knows; and even though he was fined for his actions, I don't think he can change, even if he wanted to.

We paired up as partners for a very simple reason. We think we make the best doubles team in the world.

Q. Do pro bowlers like pressure situations?

A. I don't know if they like them. I do know that it means they're in the thick of it. Because they are born gamblers, I think there is a kind of thrill in facing up to pressure, even though they all do it differently.

One of the oddest solutions I have heard is Frank Ellenburg's. He sings to himself, and usually it's a song called "We Are the Champions" by the rock group Queen.

Q. What is separation?

A. If your target on the lane is the third arrow, you can't stand on the third arrow board on the approach. Separation is the distance you allow between your standing position and where you want the ball placed on the lane to hit the target. It will vary according to the way you walk and swing.

Q. Some pros use a starting style in which the bowling arm is limp at the side. Is it worth trying?

A. Carmen Salvino started the trend. It eliminates pushaway problems and almost guarantees a straight swing. However, you must be strong enough to hold the ball there, then generate enough speed with a very brief back swing; so I feel that very few bowlers, except physically strong and experienced pros, can use this method.

Q. Do you still get nervous when you bowl on TV?

A. Every time, and so does Chris Schenkel and anybody else. Actually, you feel tense just at the beginning; then once you roll a ball, you overcome the nervousness. Most bowlers become hams after a while and love to bowl on TV. But they still get nervous.

Q. Do you think modern-day bowlers are better than the old timers?

A. No. I think all great bowlers are great. If Earl Anthony had bowled 50 years ago he would have been great; and if Jimmy Smith and Hank Marino were in their prime now, they would be great. If you're one of the best, you adjust.

In many cases, bowling events are switched to giant arenas for the finals. Here's a scene from Madison Square Garden, where two lanes were specially constructed for a tourney. The eerie effect is caused by the lights used for TV.

Q. Where I bowl the lanes are longer than other places; what should I do?

A. Lanes in some centers may look longer or shorter. I assure you, it's an optical illusion, or else we're back in the 1800s when there were no standard measurements for lanes, balls, pins, etc.

Q. What do you do about a sore hand?

A. If my hand hurts from too much bowling, I just soak it. You can use various solutions, but I would only use one recommended by a doctor or a druggist. Don Johnson used to stick his thumb in a potato. I tried it, and it felt good. In the same area, you should, if you bowl enough, develop a series of calluses, the key one being in the thumb web, with another on the palm area near the index finger; and if you use a finger-tip, on the flats of the two fingers. Always watch your callus growths. They can tell you how you're rolling the ball, because only plenty of

friction can cause the build up. If you have a callus on the back of the thumb, you're knuckling the ball, and either the span or thumb pitch is bad; or else you have a bad case of the wrong kind of squeeze.

Q. Is it true that some pro bowlers take so long because they actually can't get started?

A. Partially. There have been a number of fine bowlers who just couldn't get going; and the more they tried, the longer they took. It happens to golfers, too. It can be caused by nervous tension, and bowlers have used hypnotism and various other means to get out of it. Sometimes a simple thing such as getting into motion by rocking the ball or swinging it without disturbing the normal stance will help.

That's one side. Other bowlers are just slow.

Q. Do you have any suggestions on how bowling can be improved?

A. One way would be for more bowling proprietors to have instructors. Another would be for the big city newspapers to give bowling more space and treat bowling more like a major sport; and finally for the pros, bowling stadiums to handle crowds and bring in more gate money would be nice.

Q. What bowlers do you admire most?
A. The bowlers I respect most are the guys like Dick Weber, Carmen Salvino, Teata Semiz—bowlers who have rolled well on all the changing lane conditions. Bowlers that can win in two or three different decades are just amazing. Add Don Johnson and Dick Ritger.

   The most courageous bowler I ever knew had to be Dick Battista. He had a heart transplant and went back on the tour, and even managed to cash. He lived with his new heart for more than five years; and when he died, it was from something else, not his heart.

Q. What do you like about the pro tour, and what do you dislike?
A. I love the bowling, but I dislike the traveling, living out of a suitcase. If I could just be transported to the start of the tournament each week from my living room that would be a dream come true.

Q. Everyone keeps talking about a straight arm swing. How do you get one?
A. You can practice. Use the time-tested placement of an object, a towel, magazine, or maybe a thin newspaper beneath your arm as you go to the foul line. If the object remains under your arm, then you know your arm swing is close; if it falls, there is room for improvement. You can learn to get the ball out on the lane in the same way, by placing a towel at the foul line and making sure you don't hit it.

Q. During bowling tournaments, the fans are only a few feet away. Does that bother you?
A. Not unless they start talking too loudly or they try to talk to the bowlers. When you're a spectator, just respect the bowlers out there. They will be happy to talk to you or sign autographs when they have completed their bowling. In fact, if they talk to you or sign an autograph while bowling, they can be fined. I myself like to cool off for about ten minutes after I'm done bowling.

Q. What are your goals?
A. I don't set any specific goals as to number of tournaments I want to win. I started out to make a living, and I was lucky to make a good living; but from the first time I won a tournament my only goal has been to win every one I enter.

The three pros pictured, Teata Semiz, Marshall Holman, and Carmen Salvino, are all multiple champions. All started young, all are colorful. Semiz and Salvino continued to be major threats well into their 40s while Holman became the most controversial figure in the sport.

151

CARMEN SALVINO

WHAT THE EXPERTS
HAVE TO SAY
ABOUT MARK ROTH

Dr. George Allen (co-author of *The Encyclopedia of Strikes* and *The Encyclopedia of Spares*)

"In most cases a lane condition dictates a given line to a bowler. Not so with Mark Roth. He dictates to the lanes and often overpowers the so-called dictated line. Roth points up the fact that unorthodox is different, not wrong; what often appears to be a fault can be a great strength; and that all superstars are not traditionals.

"He proves that muscles do indeed have thought, that natural is best, that there is no such thing as a single style, that unconscious confidence is preferable to conscious paralysis by analysis.

"The lesson Mark Roth should teach every bowler is to bowl within your game, do not try to emulate someone else, learn the principles of the game, but learn how to apply them to your game and at your level.

"Roth is the greatest of our time, could be the greatest of all time."

Nelson Burton, Jr. (member of the PBA and American Bowling Congress Halls of Fame; color analyst on ABC-TV's *Pro Bowlers Tour* telecasts)

"There is little that is really odd or different about Mark Roth's game, but he has an inner looseness that is unbelievable. Every bowler seems to choke a bit or at least change something in their game when they are under pressure. Not Roth. To me he's the greatest natural talent ever, and that's the biggest secret to his success. He shows that being yourself all the time really works."

Tom Kouros (author of *Par Bowling;* consultant to pro bowlers)

"Mark Roth has it all, great hand and speed acceleration, two fine power steps, and the ability to get the ball down the lane. Never have I not seen him go through the shot, give the maximum at ball release, and follow through. His uncanny eye–hand coordination make him one of the best pocket shooters of our time.

"He has a good physical build for bowling, fine eyes, great control, and he's an intelligent bowler who makes the lane come to him. The right revolutions on the ball are important, and Roth has the right ones; but more important, his ball breaks from 2 to 6 feet before the pocket, while most others are from 8 to 12 feet. That's why he destroys the pins. He also tells you in his words or actions that he is going to beat you in any way he can, and that mental attitude enhances his physical attributes.

"If any bowler can learn how to go through the ball the way Roth does, and to get the ball down the lane in his efficient manner, they

153

have mastered two of the big steps up the ladder to better bowling.

"Right now I rate him as one of the three greatest of all time. He may wind up the greatest, and I think he could be the Arnold Palmer of bowling. He's a 10, and there are no other 10s on the tour currently. I have worked with hundreds of pro bowlers, and seldom is it that we don't find an area to work on. There is little I could do for Mark Roth, and I would never change him."

Chris Schenkel (long-time outstanding sportscaster, and play-by-play commentator on ABC's *Pro Bowlers Tour)*

"In all the great athletes I have ever covered and had contact with in my many years of sportscasting, the will and hunger to win has been apparent, the mark of the best of the best. Roth has always had that yearning to win, and I place him in the same class with Jack Nicklaus."

Larry Lichstein (author of the bowling tip column in *National Bowlers Journal;* a former pro; and the man who advises and drills bowling balls for dozens of pros in his position as PBA players' services chief)

"Mark Roth has a dynamic style which incorporates the most velocity, most power, and most natural instinct of any bowler on tour. Roth was gifted with a great body for bowling, particularly powerful thighs and legs; and he uses them perfectly. His confidence is such that he knows he is going to win every tournament he enters, and he feels that way until he either wins or loses it.

"One factor often overlooked is the fact that Roth is one of the top three spare shooters on tour, and probably the best split maker. He converts at least three splits a tournament, bouncing the pins off the side or from the pit, and that adds more than a thousand pins a year to his total.

"Any bowler can learn from Roth. Watch how he makes the most of what he's got, watch how he concentrates on every shot, never giving away a single pin through carelessness or not being set properly.

"I can sum him up simply, as a bowler and an analyst, I envy his ability."

Harry Golden (PBA tournament director who has seen Roth roll in every tournament)

"Mark Roth has such great coordination that he is naturally good at everything he does athletically. I have no doubt that if he switched hands he could quickly average better than 200, rolling left-handed.

"He has power legs, a good deep knee bend, and I feel that as long as his legs hold up he will dominate the tour. The average bowler should carefully look over Roth's finish, where he is firm, in great position to release the ball with power.

"It's often said that he intimidates his opponents personally. I don't feel that. His ball does the talking, and his ball does the scaring."

Bob Simonelli (bowler and pro shop operator to whom Roth gives credit for solving his thumb problems)

"Mark Roth's greatest asset is that he knows his own game, and he has faith in others. When he detects something that doesn't feel just right with a ball, he calls, explains what he considers the problem, then leaves it up to me or someone else he has faith in to come up with an answer. He then tries what we come up with. He never tries to get into deep explanations of what he feels he might need. All bowlers should have confidence in others to help, leaving the bowler free to concentrate almost fully on his bowling."

John Jowdy (writer; instructor who has attended more pro tournaments than any except pros or pro officials)

"Mark Roth's success is due to his speed, stuff, and accuracy. Any one of those used in the right way can be instrumental in making a fine bowler. He utilizes them all to the highest efficiency and adds an animallike instinct for attack and victory.

"One more asset, and the one any bowler can benefit from, is a simple one—the ability to listen. There are no pretensions about Roth. If you have the knowledge, he will listen to you; and so should every bowler listen to a qualified advisor, or just listen in general when bowlers are discussing the sport."

Index